POLLS

Their Use and Misuse in Politics

CHARLES W. ROLL, JR.

&

ALBERT H. CANTRIL

Basic Books, Inc., Publishers

NEW YORK / LONDON

© 1972 by Basic Books, Inc.

Library of Congress Catalog Card Number: 72–86682
SBN 465–05972–4
Manufactured in the United States of America
DESIGNED BY VINCENT TORRE

72 73 74 75   10 9 8 7 6 5 4 3 2 1

To the memory of our fathers

Foreword

WHEN President Nixon announced the mining of the harbors of North Vietnam, the White House within two days declared that his action was supported by a majority of the American people. For evidence the White House Press Secretary cited more than 20,000 telegrams and letters received in the hours following the announcement, running "five- to six-to-one" in favor of the mining, and a poll by the Opinion Research Corporation concluding that nearly three out of every four Americans backed the President. The wisdom of the escalation was thereupon sealed: "The People" had spoken; the President had to be right. Or so it seemed.

Two days later that instant White House sonar was being challenged by other blips coming back from different strata of the *vox populi*. Senator Williams of New Jersey reported that *his* mail was running overwhelmingly against the President. And Channel 13, the public television outlet in New York City, said its viewers had called to protest the mining by a nine-to-one ratio.

There were reasons for the differences, of course. The telegrams and telephone calls which inundated the White House in the hours after the President's announcement were most likely from people already disposed toward Mr. Nixon. (Immediately after one of Lyndon Johnson's fateful televised speeches, my wife called to ask what time I would be home for dinner and was promptly recorded as one of the favorable respondents to the Presidential announcement.) Senator Williams is a Democrat to whose office, rather than to his Republican counterpart, undoubtedly were to come the majority of New Jersey dissidents to Mr. Nixon's escalation. And it is highly improbable that the bedrock audience of Channel 13 in the metropolitan New York area harbors hawkish tendencies toward the war in Vietnam.

Furthermore, even if the initial public response to the President's statement was in the first hours generally favorable to the mining, the White House would have been amiss to take much comfort from the fact. The whole relationship between public opinion and the war in Vietnam has been to confirm that instinct among Presidential counselors which might be translated: "When in doubt, act." The theory is that the public will forgive a bad Presidential decision sooner than no decision at all, or at least it will forget a bad decision when hope is aroused by a later, more promising, one. Almost anything our Presidents have done which appeared to be moving the war to an end has been tentatively greeted by approving opinion polls. Thus, President Johnson's ratings increased sharply when he ordered the long bombing pause in December, 1965. A month later, disillusionment set in as the pause did not seem to be ending the war, and public opinion once more began to slip away from the President. But immediately upon his resumption of the bombing, Mr. Johnson's stock was up again—at least temporarily.

We are beseiged on every front by polls which say this and that, but about the meaning of polls and the techniques by which they are taken, there is a dearth of understanding. The root of the word once described the broad end of a bludgeoning tool, one used to hammer and shape other objects. It is a fitting symbol of the use to which polls can be put, as Lyndon Johnson

Charles W. Roll, Jr., and Albert H. Cantril are co-authors of *Hopes and Fears of the American People.*

Orren Jack Turner

Mr. Roll is President of Political Surveys and Analyses, Inc., which has counted among its clients Nelson Rockefeller of New York, Richard Hughes of New Jersey, and Senator Howard Baker of Tennessee. He is also the Study Director of the Gallup Organization, where he has conducted surveys for *The New York Times, The Wall Street Journal, Philadelphia Bulletin,* and many others.

Fabian Bachrach

Albert H. Cantril is an independent consultant in political and social research. After receiving his Ph.D. in Political Science from MIT, he joined the White House staff, serving as research aide to Bill D. Moyers. He has been a consultant to the former Bureau of the Budget and to the Division of Behavioral Science of the National Academy of Science. He also served for two years in the Department of State.

demonstrated in 1964 when he repeatedly whisked from his pocket the latest poll showing how completely he would bury Goldwater. Whether a bandwagon existed or not, President Johnson wanted to create the impression that one was rolling in an effort to persuade Republicans to desert Goldwater and go all the way with LBJ.

All of this is to suggest the coquetry of public opinion polling and to welcome this book by Albert H. Cantril and Charles W. Roll, Jr. It is a layman's guide, not a technical treatise, although Cantril and Roll are both authorities in the field. Their names are less familiar on the public marquee than Harris and Gallup, but they are men of long and important experience in the study of public opinion. Cantril served with me at the White House; his assignment was to interpret what the polls reported and to analyze the meaning of the fundamental structures of attitudes and prejudice, the underlying depths of what Macaulay called "the flux and reflux" of public opinion. There was no way to flatter or intimidate "Tad" Cantril into betraying his professional judgment in order to give the President a better night's sleep.

Charlie Roll is study director in The Gallup Organization and president of Political Surveys and Analyses, whose clients include Democratic and Republican politicians. I know him as a man who would tell the Emperor not only that he is naked but that the polls which had influenced him to accept nudity as the public fashion were in fact taken in a nudist colony. In other words, Charlie Roll would say, consider the sample. It is this kind of advice which he and Cantril bring to this practical guide to poll watching.

I have considerable respect for the honest professionals of polling. Partly, this respect grows out of a conviction arrived at in government that knowing what the public believes is essential to leadership. "As the happiness of the people is the sole end of government," the Council of Massachusetts Bay proclaimed in 1774, "so the *consent of the people* is the only foundation of it, in reason, morality, and the natural fitness of things." One needs to know what people believe before he can fashion laws to which they will volunteer their consent or before he can try to persuade them that they are wrong and should change their opinions. Is there a better case study than Vietnam of what can happen to the well-being of a nation when its government insists on pursuing a policy the people essentially refuse to accept as wise or necessary?

This is not to imply that because a majority of the people say something is so, it is so: whoring after that one plus fifty has reduced many a momentarily popular "leader" to the status of a footnote in a history book. It is to admit that the pressure of public opinion, in J. R. Lowell's description, "is like the pressure of the atmosphere—you can't see it, but all the same, it is sixteen pounds to the square inch." In a democracy this pressure begs to be explored and understood. But so do the techniques by which the "pressure of public opinion" is examined. Otherwise, in an era of mass communication, public opinion can become not what people think but what politicians and pollsters say they think.

Against this potentially grave assault on the political process Cantril and Roll warn and instruct, and in addition to throwing light on the techniques by which we as a people are being constantly assayed, they strike a moral and social concern that could hardly be more timely.

BILL D. MOYERS

Preface

THE idea for this book grew out of our participation in the preparation of a series of programs on public opinion research for the Nebraska Educational Television Council on Higher Education, located on the campus of the University of Nebraska at Lincoln.

The experience upon which we have drawn in this book has been particularly enriched by four men. Paul K. Perry, to whom the remarkable accuracy of the Gallup Poll since 1952 must be credited, taught us a deep appreciation for the importance of resourcefulness and attention to detail in accurately measuring public sentiment. We owe a debt to Archibald M. Crossley, whose imagination and integrity set a high standard for those of us in the field today. We have been inspired by the breadth of interest and quality of research of the late Hadley Cantril. And we have learned from Lloyd A. Free, whose flare for turning opinion data into political strategy is unsurpassed. Had these men ever collaborated on a political survey it would have been a classic.

We are very grateful to Dr. George Gallup, whose name has become synonymous with polls, for allowing us to use freely data from the Gallup Poll and from whom we have benefited through numerous conversations over the years.

Our story is supported by illustrative material we have fortunately been able to include. Much of this information was gathered in behalf of a number of individuals: Governor Nelson A. Rockefeller, who has been particularly sensitive to and supportive of meaningful survey research; U.S. Senator Howard Baker; Congressman Ogden Reid; former Governors Robert Meyner and Richard Hughes of New Jersey, and Raymond Shafer of Pennsylvania; and former Lt. Governor Richard Ristine of Indiana.

In the preparation of this book we have communicated with numerous people. Among them were: Robert T. Bower, Hugh Branson, Martin Clancy, Charles M. Cooke, Jr., John O. Davies, 3rd, Morgan J. Doughton, the Honorable James A. Farley, L. Richard Guylay, Calvin Kytle, Stacy B. Lloyd, Philip Meyer, Bill D. Moyers, James M. Nicholson, Barry J. Nova, Steven Rivkin, Jack Rosenthal, Richard Scammon, Michael J. Stap, and Ted Van Dyk.

And our thanks go to the patience of Helen Keeler, who typed drafts of the manuscript.

C.W.R., JR.

A.H.C.

Contents

Contents

☞ POLLS ☜

1

Polling: The Fifth Estate

Wonder grows where knowledge fails.
TACITUS

ON the evening of October 31, 1968, President Lyndon Johnson made his historic announcement that all United States bombing of North Vietnam was to be stopped. Within forty-eight hours the campaign headquarters of Richard Nixon had available to it a detailed analysis of how the American people had reacted.

In the waning hours of the Presidential campaign, this information could have been vital. What benefit had accrued to Mr. Nixon's opponent Vice President Humphrey? Would the Republican candidate need to make a statement, and, if so, what form should it take? For this kind of information the Nixon campaign was willing to pay a tidy sum. It is known that the polling budget for the Nixon campaign amounted to at least $584,000. Roughly one-third of this sum was spent prior to the Miami Convention, and the balance afterwards.

The Republicans were not alone, however, in their reliance upon polls. The polling operation for the Democrats was not so ambitious as that in the Republican camp and did not start until after the Democratic Convention. Nonetheless, a total of $282,000 was spent for polls. Add to this, the sums spent by Governor Wallace and the other aspirants in the preconvention months, and the total tops $1.5 million spent for polling on the Presidential race alone.

By conservative estimate, a total of 1,200 individual polls

3

were privately commissioned by candidates for office at all levels in the 1968 election. This represents an overall total expenditure for privately commissioned polls in 1968 of about $6 million.[1]

What the impact of these polls was on the individual races would be hard to determine. The fact is, however, that the polling technique was obviously perceived as a necessary ingredient for a successful campaign. It is said that those most prone to rely upon polls, in mapping their campaign strategy, budget from 3 to 5 percent of their overall campaign funds to this kind of research.

The privately commissioned polls were not the only ones followed. The regularly published polls of George Gallup and Louis Harris were also closely watched. Candidates would clamor for "advance" notice of how their standing fluctuated. Poll results, if encouraging, tended to be believed and flaunted. If discouraging, the results were discounted or disputed.

Among those who watched the polls most closely were the potential contributors to the campaigns. They kept a keen eye on these published polls for early hints as to which candidate was the likely winner. It is known, for example, that the Humphrey-Muskie campaign suffered a dollar deficiency early after the Democratic Convention, and it is alleged that this was due in large part to poor showings in the polls. In early July, Humphrey had held a five percentage point lead over Richard Nixon in the Gallup Poll. By late that month, Humphrey began to slip and ran two points behind Nixon. The trend against Humphrey continued, and, just prior to the Democratic Convention in late August, he was down by sixteen points. As Humphrey aides told us, this greatly complicated fund-raising immediately after the Convention. By late September, the margin had changed little, and funds were still short. As a result, two weeks of television spots had to be cut—at the height of the campaign— and Robert Short, Treasurer of the Democratic National Committee, launched a massive loan drive.

4

By early October, Humphrey began to regain his strength against Nixon in the polls, narrowing the margin to twelve points, and campaign contributions were more forthcoming. As of the third week in October, Humphrey had closed the gap further to eight points and was ultimately defeated in the election by less than one percentage point.[2]

Overall, the Nixon campaign had twice the funds available for media activities as did the Democrats. In the last weeks of the campaign, however, when the Democrats' financial situation had improved, both sides spent about the same. Humphrey's early drop in the polls cannot alone explain the initial financial troubles of the Democrats, but it certainly did not help! When the polls began to look up for Humphrey, so did everything else. This explains, in part, Humphrey's sudden resurgence.

Again in 1972, the polls were closely watched. Would Edmund Muskie be able to hold on as the front-runner? If Edward Kennedy did not run, what other candidate would profit most from the additional backing of Kennedy partisans? Would Hubert Humphrey be able to overcome the legacies of the 1968 Chicago Convention and the Vietnam policies of the Johnson Administration and reestablish himself as a viable candidate? Would Governor Wallace hurt the Democrats more than the Republicans? Surely had the polls not thrown a wet blanket on their candidacies, Senators Harris and Hughes might have been tempted to hold on a bit longer, and contributions to sustain their campaigns would have been more forthcoming.

☞ Polling Comes of Age ☜

It should come as no surprise that the polling technique has caught on in American politics. It is a logical extension of our political tradition. Not only are we told ours is a "government of the people, by the people, and for the people," but one of the basic trends in the evolution of our constitutional system has been the expansion of opportunities for public participation in the political process.

In the early days of the Republic, only property owners were enfranchised. Gradually, the property requirements were lowered. Then, with the Fifteenth Amendment (which made it illegal to prevent a person from voting on the basis of race), Negroes were given the right to vote—on paper at least. It was not until the Twenty-Fourth Amendment was passed a century later that the obstacle of the poll tax, which disenfranchised so many Negroes, was outlawed. As recently as 1920, the Nineteenth Amendment extended suffrage to women. And the trend continued in the Twenty-Third Amendment, which allowed residents of the District of Columbia to vote in Presidential elections, and finally in the recent eighteen-year-old vote provision found in the Twenty-Sixth Amendment.

To our knowledge, the Frenchman J. Hector St. John de Crevecoeur was the first person to gather systematically information about the American public. Traveling as James St. John, he traversed the frontier in the late eighteenth century. His approach was remarkably deliberate: "Whenever I hear of any new settlement, I pay it a visit once or twice a year, on purpose to observe the different steps each settler takes; the gradual improvements; the different tempers of each family, on which their prosperity in a great measure depends; their different modifications of industry; their ingenuity and contrivance; for being all poor, their life requires sagacity."[3]

He recounts an interview with "an honest Scotch Hebridean" in 1774 in Pennsylvania—typical of his approach:

Well, Friend, how do you do now; I am come fifty odd miles on purpose to see you; how do you go on with your new cutting and slashing?

Very well, good sir; we learn to use of the axe bravely, we shall make it out; we have a belly full of victuals every day; our cows run about and come home full of milk; our hogs get fat of themselves in the woods. Oh, this is good country! God bless the King and William Penn; we shall do very well by and by, if we keep our health.

Your log-house looks neat and light. Where did you get these shingles?

One of our neighbours is a New England man, and he showed us how to split them out of chestnut-trees. Now for a barn, but all in good time; here are fine trees to build it with. . . .

What did you give for your land?

Thirty-five shillings per acre, payable in seven years.

How many acres have you got?

A hundred and fifty.

That is not enough to begin with; is not your land pretty hard to clear?

Yes sir, hard enough, but it would be harder still if it was already cleared, for then we should have no timber, and I love the woods much; the land is nothing without them.

Have not you found out any bees yet?

No, sir; and if we had, we should not know what to do with them. . . .[4]

And just as so many researchers today feel after such an excursion, de Crevecoeur asked, "Is it not better to contemplate under these humble roofs the rudiments of future wealth and population than to behold the accumulated bundles of litigious papers in the office of a lawyer?"[5]

The first report of political fact-finding to measure candidate strength was recorded in the July 24, 1824 issue of the *Harrisburg Pennsylvanian,* in which a straw vote was taken at Wilmington, Delaware, "without Discrimination of Parties." This Wilmington Presidential Poll indicated majority support for Andrew Jackson, who received 335 votes as opposed to 169 for John Quincy Adams, 19 for Henry Clay, and 9 for William Crawford. This Jackson lead in the sampling did not prevent the Delaware legislature—which had the power to select that state's Presidential electors—from selecting men who would

7

support Crawford in the electoral college. The poll may have been an influence, however, when it fell to Delaware's lone Congressman Louis McLane, to place his state in the Jackson column in preference to Adams in the House of Representatives vote after the electoral college had failed to give any candidate a majority of its votes.

In August of the same year, the *Raleigh Star* undertook to canvass political meetings held in North Carolina "at which the sense of the people was taken." Jackson, who read law in North Carolina, received 3,428 votes as opposed to Adams' 470, and Crawford's 358. Jackson carried the state that fall, although by a considerably smaller margin, and received the full support of North Carolina's representatives in the electoral college and, later, in the House of Representatives.[6]

The next glimpse of an early device to record pre-election preferences has recently been mentioned by the American historian, Daniel Boorstin, in *The Americans: The National Experience*. Citizens traveling around the country at this time voluntarily recorded their Presidential preferences in the register of the hotel at which they were staying. "Each person entered the name of the Presidential candidate for whom he intended to vote."[7] The English traveler, J. S. Buckingham, noted of the register, for example, at Ball's Hotel in Brownsville, Pennsylvania in 1840, "Thus the column contained the entries of Harrison against the world—Van Buren for ever—Henry Clay, The Pride of Kentucky—Little Van, The Magician—Old Tippecanoe, and no sub-treasury—The Farmer of North Bend— Hurrah for Jackson—Van Buren again—Log Cabin and Hard Cider—and so on page after page. In this way some attempt is made to ascertain the strength of the parties; the best is most imperfect."[8]

Aside from measuring the preferences of the traveling class only, this name-anyone-you-want approach resulted in support for two men—Clay and Jackson—who were not on any ballot in 1840. Of significance, however, is this early evidence of eager enthusiasm on the part of Americans to identify with a candidate publicly and even voluntarily.

The first recorded poll for a state contest was conducted by an enterprising newspaperman in Mississippi in 1851. An assistant editor of the *Natchez Courier* isolated seventeen critical counties where he felt the outcome was in doubt. In each county, he interviewed several dozen men eligible to vote. If, on the basis of interviewing, a clear trend developed, he moved on to the next county. If it did not, he interviewed until the proportions stabilized. In all, he conducted about 800 interviews and correctly predicted the direction and approximate margin in fifteen out of the seventeen counties. The overall popular vote results fell within two points of his calculations. According to Walter E. Simonson of the Burroughs Corporation, to whom we are indebted for this historical morsel, the antisecessionist views of the governor, Henry S. Foote, had become so unpopular by 1854 that he had to resign from office. Thus, thanks to this early sampling plus some historical interpretation, we are able to date the shift from dominant antisecessionist sentiment to prosecessionist sentiment in Mississippi as occurring sometime between 1851 and 1854.

To our knowledge, the first attempt to assess public opinion systematically in the early days of this century was made by Tammany Hall. Tammany workers would fan out across New York City to get a reading on the public's leanings at election time. Workers positioned themselves at bridges and other key spots asking people their candidate preferences. The effort was so sophisticated that the workers at each location were changed daily to reduce bias and insure as honest and accurate a headcount as was possible. Thus, Tammany had what it regarded as a reliable day-to-day reading of the election situation during the campaign period.[9]

However, the first candidate for public office ever to have the benefit of a public opinion poll was Mrs. Alex Miller, who in 1932 was elected the first woman Secretary of State in Iowa. She had been approached by a young man interested in trying out, in a political campaign, a sampling technique he had developed as a Ph.D. candidate to assess readership of stories and advertisements in the newspapers. A poll was done, and he found Mrs. Miller had a good chance of winning and pinpointed the approaching Democratic sweep in Republican Iowa. The young man was her son-in-law, George H. Gallup.

It was the election of 1936 that brought the new "scientific" polls to life. These polls were to be contrasted to the notoriety of the soundings of the *Literary Digest,* which had mailed out ten million ballots across the country. Of those ballots, roughly one-fifth were returned, and their tabulation indicated that Roosevelt would obtain only 40.9 percent of the vote and be defeated by Landon. Young Gallup had the audacity not only to predict that the *Digest* would be wrong, but also to predict Roosevelt's reelection with 55.7 percent of the vote. The final returns gave the incumbent 62.5 percent. Also remarkably close in these early days were the surveys of Archibald Crossley and the *Fortune* poll, just begun by Elmo Roper, predicting a Roosevelt victory with a 53.8 percent and 61.7 percent respectively.[10]

Four years later Franklin Roosevelt was to be the first President to have a regular flow of polling information coming into his office. In the spring of 1940 he asked Professor Hadley Cantril of Princeton University's psychology department to measure the trends of public opinion about the war in Europe. Cantril initially asked questions through the facilities of George Gallup but later set up his own polling capability. With support from the Rockefeller Foundation, he established the Office of Public Opinion Research at Princeton to explore the techniques of opinion polling and to begin to compile an archive of poll findings.[11]

Most of Cantril's work for President Roosevelt had been financed by Gerard B. Lambert, a retired industrialist living in Princeton. Lambert himself became interested in the polling technique and was the first to conduct research for a Presidential candidate. In 1940, he oversaw polling done for Thomas E. Dewey, then the District Attorney of Manhattan. Despite his success in several primaries, Dewey was overwhelmed by the Willkie blitz at the Republican Convention. Lambert continued his work, polling for Willkie, who it turned out was less appreciative of polling information than Dewey. This was exemplified by his excessive campaigning in the South, where polls indicated there was little chance of his picking up strength.

Excepting Mrs. Miller in Iowa, the first statewide candidate to use privately commissioned polls was Robert Hendrickson of New Jersey, in his primary battle for the Republican gubernatorial nomination and subsequent unsuccessful general election bid. This work, too, was done by Lambert.[12]

Dwight Eisenhower, as well, had polls available to him. He not only watched private polls conducted during his campaign by Archibald Crossley and later by Lambert, but he also had a keen interest in reports on the state of worldwide public opinion that were turned in to him weekly by Lloyd A. Free.[13] In the 1960 Presidential campaign, polls became more respectable as both sides set up extensive polling operations. The Nixon campaign relied heavily upon polls turned in by George Gallup's early associate, Claude Robinson; and it was the Kennedy campaign that brought Louis Harris to prominence.

☞ Need to Know ☜

Clearly, "the polls" are here to stay—and to stay in a rather major way. If the press and mass media can be termed "the Fourth Estate" of government, then the polling establishment is easily a candidate to become "the Fifth Estate." Polling now touches the core of our national political process—integrated intimately into almost every aspect of its workings. Even in the determination of which Presidential candidates should become eligible for protection by the Secret Service, for example, a bipartisan committee devised a formula based upon poll findings. It stated that any announced candidate who receives at least 5 percent in a Gallup or Harris poll is entitled to protection and that any undeclared candidate who receives 20 percent or more would also be eligible.[14]

When any new institution establishes for itself so firm a footing, serious questions naturally arise about its scope, its procedure, and its integrity. Can the polls be trusted? Do they serve or abuse the public interest? Is the public informed enough to be taken seriously at every turn in decision-making? What makes for a good poll?

As with any aspect of national political life that comes into its own so quickly, there are excesses. They are found in the leader who slavishly tailors his posture to poll results. They are found, too, in the poll-taker who sells his wares only to abuse a client's confidence.

Exemplary of how far the excesses can go are the following episodes known to have transpired in recent years.

In a Senate primary contest, two polling firms were bidding for a client's business. When a decision became imminent in favor of one firm, the head of the other firm took the client aside to offer a service no one else could offer. He would provide two surveys: one for use with the press for publicity and fund-raising purposes and one to report on how things really stood in the state.

In one of the larger Eastern states, a poll-taker amassed poll findings and manipulated them to exaggerate the unpopularity of an incumbent governor. He then threatened the release of these findings to the press unless a poll was commissioned through his organization. In another state, this same poll-taker did, indeed, release the alleged unfavorable findings when the client switched from his firm to another firm.

In 1970, the *New York Daily News'* Straw Poll showed incumbent Charles Goodell running a poor third in the Senate race. According to a public statement by an aide to the former Senator, shortly after the Straw Poll was published, the Senator's staff was contacted by a polling firm asking if there would be any interest in purchasing a poll which would show Goodell ahead.

A businessman in one of the Southwestern states was contemplating a bid for the gubernatorial nomination and commissioned a private poll. Some weeks later he was startled to learn that highly sensitive findings in his "confidential" poll had been leaked to one of the national leaders of his party from his own state. The poll-taker had passed these findings along in the apparent hope of stimulating business with the party nationally.

Such episodes are the exception, not the rule. But they do highlight the ease with which politicians and the public can be unwittingly taken in by "the polls." With each additional insult, the entire polling community suffers, and its integrity is increasingly questioned.

This book has been written with the conviction that the time has come for a close look at polling—as both a process and an institution. It is written by two practitioners of the art in the belief that it is only people in the field who are alert to where things can go astray and what should be guarded against. At the same time, it is only they who can highlight what the potential uses—as well as limitations—of the polling technique are.

Privately commissioned polls have become a landmark on the American political scene. The polls have truly come of age. Polling is now an industry in its own right, serving not only candidates for public office, but also a wide panoply of clients ranging from organized labor to business to the many lobbies and special interest groups.

With the new technologies available through computers, the

potential capabilities of polling are staggering. But the question that haunts the observer is, "Where will it all lead?" What of the sanctity of the individual—his predispositions as well as his privacy? What about a leader's role as persuader and educator—not the slavish mimic of the computer printout?

As the polling fraternity adjusts to its new visibility and influence, so too will the public adjust and learn how to live with the polls. The excesses of the past are unfortunate, but, hopefully, the polling practitioner will respond to the affront by policing himself. What the ultimate judgment will be as to the merits of polling is hard to foresee. However, it is only through greater understanding of the polling technique that the public and the politicians will be able to come to a fair appraisal for themselves. It is toward this end that this book has been written.

As we shall point out, the public opinion poll, responsibly used, can greatly strengthen the democratic process by providing "the people" yet another way of making their views known—particularly between elections. But, as we shall also point out, polling employed in an irresponsible manner can be most injurious as special interests misrepresent the public interest and as demagogic politicians exploit the many legitimate and deep-rooted concerns of the people.

We do not intend this as a text or how-to-do-it manual. Our purpose is solely to acquaint the reader with some of the intricacies of political polling and to describe the setting in which the polls can be most responsibly and beneficially used in our free society. We hope to provide a backdrop against which the politician, the press, and the public may judge "the polls" that are ever more omnipresent in our national political life.

Notes

1. Herbert E. Alexander, *Financing the 1968 Election* (Lexington: D. C. Heath & Co., 1971), pp. 113–116. These figures indicate that an average of $5,000 was spent on each of the 1,200 polls. This figure is probably a bit low since poll costs can range from a couple of thousand dollars for a small survey to upwards of $50,000 for a comprehensive survey.

2. The trend according to the Gallup Poll:

INTERVIEWING DATES	NIXON	HUMPHREY	WALLACE	UNDECIDED
April 6-10	43%	34%	9%	14%
May 4-8	39	36	14	11
May 25-29	36	42	14	8
June 15-16	37	42	14	7
June 29-July 3	35	40	16	9
July 19-21	40	38	16	6
July 31	40	38	16	6
August 21	45	29	18	8
Democratic Convention				
September 3-7	43	31	19	7
September 20-22	43	28	21	8
September 27-30	44	29	20	7
October 3-12	43	31	20	6
October 17-21	44	36	15	5
October 31-November 2	42	40	14	4

3. J. Hector St. John de Crevecoeur, *Letters from an American Farmer* (New York: Signet Classic, 1963), p. 80.

4. Ibid., pp. 80–81.

5. Ibid., p. 81.

6. See George Gallup and Saul Forbes Rae, *The Pulse of Democracy* (New York: Simon and Schuster, 1940), pp. 34–35.

7. Quoted in Daniel J. Boorstin, *The Americans: The National Experience* (New York: Vintage Books, 1964), p. 140.

8. Ibid.

9. Recalled in Charles Roll's interview with James A. Farley.

10. For a detailed account of this period, see Daniel Katz and Hadley Cantril, "Public Opinion Polls," *Sociometry* 1 (1937): pp. 155–179.

11. See Hadley Cantril, *The Human Dimension: Experiences in Policy Research* (New Brunswick: Rutgers University Press, 1967); see

also James MacGregor Burns, *The Soldier of Freedom* (New York: Harcourt, Brace, Jovanovich, 1970), pp. 41, 112, 280–281.

12. For Lambert's own recollections of these studies, see Gerard B. Lambert, *All Out of Step* (Garden City: Doubleday, 1956).

13. The studies sponsored by Lambert were designed and executed by Joseph E. Bachelder of Princeton, New Jersey.

14. Reported in *The Washington Post,* January 28, 1972.

2

Unfortunate Uses of Polls In Politics

> Those [polls] that come out good for
> you, those are the good polls; those
> that come out bad for the candidate,
> those are the unscientific ones: so
> saith the politicians.
>
> HUBERT HUMPHREY

INCREASINGLY, it is assumed that to be "with it"—part of
the new politics—a candidate for public office must retain his
own private pollster. However, all too often the interest and
enthusiasm in polls far outdistances the understanding of how
polls can play a meaningful role in politics.

Polls are political intelligence. However, as with all forms of
intelligence, what is learned depends upon the care with which
the information is gathered and the sophistication with which it
is interpreted. The percentages in which poll results are reported
are vivid and often tend to become realities in their own right.
Yet the percentages that are reported are nothing more than
responses to specific questions, asked of specific portions of the
population, for specific purposes.

Thus, it is not enough simply to go out and "take a poll." The
polling technique is employed in the practical everyday of
politics in many ways and for many purposes. Polls differ in their
utility in a number of respects. Some are more closely tailored to
the unique needs of a candidate or political situation than others.
Some achieve a greater economy than others in terms of what is

17

learned for the dollar spent. Some provide a better basis for determination of alternative strategies and specific actions.

In this and the next chapter, we shall outline some of the more common uses to which polls are put. This chapter will present some of the more regrettable uses of the polls. We feel these uses are "regrettable" for a number of reasons. They tend to be short-sighted by stressing the surface measurement of opinion to the neglect of more basic measures, which are of greater use in helping to map out campaign strategy. In the extreme, these uses can be injurious to the democratic process by abetting the misrepresentation of what is on the public's mind.

The next chapter will focus on some of the more meaningful uses of polls in politics and demonstrate how the polls can play an affirmative role in the political process.

☞ **To Run or Not to Run?** ☜

That is the question for which many candidates look to the polls in the hope of finding an answer. The results to questions which pit one candidate against another—the so-called "trial heats"—are those most reported by the press and those to which the political client first turns when reading a poll he has commissioned.

Yet, perhaps no other findings from a political poll are more ephemeral. Since specific candidate choice questions are usually asked for the first time before a campaign begins, the results from them usually do not provide a realistic assessment of the potential strength of the candidates. The nonincumbent usually is less well-known, and it is not until the campaign is in full swing that the public becomes really aware of him.

Basing a decision whether or not to run on these early trial heat results can be folly. Take the case of Tennessee in 1966. In the Senate race, the well-known Governor Frank Clement held a twenty percentage point margin over his lesser known Republican opponent Howard Baker in a poll conducted in December 1965. However, as Baker became better known his strength picked up to the point where he defeated Clement in the election by a margin of over ten points. (See Table 2–1.)

TABLE 2-1

	DECEMBER 1965 (POLL)	SEPTEMBER 1966 (POLL)	NOVEMBER 1966 (ELECTION)
Baker	30%	54%	55.7%
Clement	50	46	44.3
Undecided	20	—	—

Howard Baker might well have been dissuaded from making the run for Senate in 1966 by the lopsidedness of the early trial heat figures. Today, however, Baker is the most popular political figure among voters of the state. Poll results show him more popular than any other figure, including men such as Nixon, Agnew, Humphrey, Muskie, Wallace, and the like. Had he dropped out in 1966, the Tennessee electorate would now be deprived of the Senator they now so strongly endorse.

Bias in a precampaign trial heat measurement can also occur against the incumbent or better-known potential candidate, particularly when he has taken actions which are unpopular with the voters. However, once the campaign is under way, and he has an opportunity to explain the reasons for his actions and to recount the accomplishments of his tenure, the voters become more favorably impressed.

Seven months prior to election day in 1966, Governor Nelson Rockefeller, according to poll results, was running nearly two-to-one behind New York City Council President Frank O'Connor. As the campaign developed, however, the Governor rose steadily and O'Connor dropped. (See Table 2–2.) Much the same thing occurred in 1970, when Rockefeller was running 9 points behind Arthur Goldberg, six months before the election—Rockefeller receiving 35 percent to Goldberg's 44 percent. By election day, the Governor was informed by his poll takers in Princeton that he would receive 53 percent of the vote with a maximum of 42 percent for Goldberg and 5 to 7 percent for Conservative Paul Adams. The election results turned out to be 52.6 percent for Rockefeller, 40.4 percent for Goldberg, and 7.0 percent for Adams.

TABLE 2-2

	APRIL 1966 (POLL)	EARLY OCTOBER 1966 (POLL)	LATE OCTOBER 1966 (POLL)	NOVEMBER 1966 (ELECTION)
Rockefeller	29%	35%	40%	44.8%
O'Connor	56	35	34	38.3
Roosevelt	Not asked	10	12	8.4
Adams	Not asked	6	6	8.5
Undecided & other	15	14	8	—

Had Rockefeller decided to avoid the uphill battle these private polls foreshadowed and bow out, he would never have become the man to serve as Governor of New York longer than anyone else since the days of George Clinton.

Decisions with respect to primary races are also often based upon early poll findings. In *The New York Times* of December 5, 1967, for example, it was reported:

Mr. Duncan said that public opinion polls had a major influence on his decision to oppose Mr. Morse (then Senator from Oregon). Two polls released by his supporters this year showed him running well ahead of the Senator.

Voter opinion in primary election situations tends to be more volatile than in the general election because the stabilizing influence of party loyalty is not working to cut down shifts between candidates. This proved to be the case in Oregon as opinion shifted and Morse carried the primary against his challenger. (See Table 2–3.)

TABLE 2-3

	JANUARY 1967* (POLL)	JULY 1967* (POLL)	MAY 1968 (ELECTION)
Morse	34%	35%	49.0%
Duncan	59	58	46.3
Undecided & other	7	7	4.7 (McAlmond)

*Reported in *New York Times*, December 5, 1967.

Despite much evidence concerning the pitfalls of acting on the basis of early poll results, a full year ahead of the 1972 elections, the press was emphasizing the importance of early polls in candidate decisions of whether to run. Kevin Phillips wrote in *The New York Times Magazine* on November 14, 1971:

If by late spring 1972 President Nixon is facing a close race and Spiro Agnew is a clear drag, the Vice President would solve things himself by stepping aside. . . . But Agnew could wind up gaining renomination in 1972 under (the) circumstance . . . in which ris-- ing Nixon-Agnew poll ratings convince the President that the safest thing is to keep his Vice President rather than rock the boat by offending conservatives.

Or consider the following two excerpts from *Newsweek,* the first dated December 6, 1971, the second a week later:

Even Miami's (Mayor) Kennedy (a Humphrey supporter) favors waiting to "fight another day" if polls show Humphrey doing badly (in Florida).

POLLS

Last week (Senator Henry) Jackson pronounced the state (New Hampshire) "Muskie country" and canceled out of the March 7 primary entirely. . . . Some of his campaign strategists thought he could win enough votes to embarrass Muskie in the Maine Senator's geopolitical backyard. But early polls showed Jackson trailing badly.

Thus, candidates and commentators apparently are still placing too much credence in these kinds of transitory and superficial data.

We do not want to leave the impression, however, that poll findings may not be important in the decision of whether or not a candidate should run. While we are not sanguine that the trial heat figures provide any reliable base for such a decision, other kinds of survey data can be produced at early stages that will help. Specifically, surveys can help determine how well a candidate identified with a particular issue might run in a state. Is the unknown potential candidate a man with a business background who opposes wage and price controls? A survey can determine how favorably the public might view the idea of a businessman going into politics and how much they agree with his stand on the wage and price control issue. Or, is the unknown candidate a former state commissioner of urban affairs planning to run against an incumbent Senator who is extremely active in matters pertaining to the problems of the elderly? A survey can determine how important urban affairs are in the public's view in contrast to problems of the elderly.

In this way, one can get around the problem of assessing the potential strength of the unknown potential candidate. But in most races it is personality that is usually particularly important, and there is no sure-fire way to measure the potential draw of an unknown.

Beyond the fact that trial heat figures are an unsound basis for decisions of whether to contest an election, there is the philosophical consideration that the voters should not be deprived of learning about the lesser known candidate who shows up poorly in a poll and of making up their own minds about him. Many are the capable men whom the voters never see in politics because they are overpowered in the early trial heats. If we are concerned with improving the quality of individuals who seek public office, this early decision-making stage is certainly one to watch very carefully.

☞ A Private Poll Showed . . . ☜

The newspapers are filled with stories of what the private polls show. Seldom is there enough information about the polls reported to evaluate their significance: sample size, questions, population surveyed, etc. Doubt always lingers as to the completeness of the reported findings and what the intentions of the source of the leak were.

Nonetheless, leaked polls do make for good reading, and they do often have an impact far beyond what they merit. Among those most impressed by leaked polls are potential campaign contributors. As Leonard Hall, Chairman of the Republican National Committee during the Eisenhower Administration, put it: "If no one else [does], politicians and spenders read polls. The big contributors like to know where their man stands, and, just like at the two-dollar window, no one likes to put his money on a loser."[1] In 1968, the Humphrey-for-President drive suffered a dollar deficiency because the early Gallup and Harris polls showed Nixon comfortably ahead —even though Humphrey was to steadily narrow the gap. Candidate Nixon was quoted in the spring of that year as saying: "When the polls go good for me, the cash register really rings."[2]

This can backfire, as it did in New Hampshire in 1972 when polls showed Edmund Muskie so far ahead that campaign contributions dropped off, potential contributors apparently feeling things were going so well that no additional resources were needed.

The fundamental issue is raised again of how the public's interest can be protected by ensuring that a range of candidates from which to choose is presented—not just those that look like good bets to potential contributors. The most effective antidote for this insult to the democratic process is greater understanding on the part of contributors about the probable changes in early trial heat findings as campaigns wear on so that they will not be lulled into commitments by the leaked opinion soundings passed on by political lieutenants.

The leaking of favorable poll results also tends to bring about better coverage of a candidacy by the press. The cherished assignment for the newsman in a campaign is to cover the most likely winner. McGovern forces in early 1972 complained bitterly that simply because of the Senator's poor showing in the polls it was next to impossible to obtain press coverage of his candidacy equal to that of Senators Muskie or Kennedy—even though McGovern had announced long ago and had taken a forthright stand on most of the controversial issues. The same thing happens even in state races, as was seen in the 1969 gubernatorial race in New Jersey when reporters flocked to the soon-to-be victorious Cahill campaign tour, leaving the Meyner camp in droves.

Leaked poll results can have direct political consequences, even when the alleged poll has not been professionally conducted. Back in 1952 at the height of the battle for the Republican Presidential nomination, leaked poll findings probably had much to do with the Eisenhower-Nixon ticket that ultimately emerged. The critical California delegation was committed by law to Earl Warren until he released delegates to vote their own preferences. Then Senator Richard Nixon, a leading member of the delegation, upset the Warren supporters as well as some Taft supporters by releasing the results of a survey he had conducted. As the episode is recounted by Leo Katcher:

> What angered the Warren people even more was the notorious questionnaire which Nixon sent out of his office, under Congressional frank, to some 23,000 of his campaign contributors [and precinct workers] asking them who they believed would be the "strongest possible Republican nominee." This was almost a "have-you-stopped-beating-your-wife" question, for many who might prefer Warren, or even Taft, as the candidate, could, in all honesty, say they believed Eisenhower was the strongest of the lot. When the results came in, they favored Eisenhower by a large margin. It was Nixon's intention to publicize this poll, but reaction from Warren and other Californians was so adverse that, instead of forthright publication, the results were allowed to "leak."[3]

The most heinous leak of favorable polling data has as its purpose the swaying of sufficient portions of the electorate to guarantee victory on election day. We find this "heinous" not because of the actual effect—which we believe to be nil—but because it betokens a kind of naïveté no sophisticated candidate for high office should evidence.

Why is it so many politicians believe that poll results will induce people to cast their ballots for the leading candidate in the polls? Irving Crespi, Executive Vice President of the Gallup Organization, answers the question well:

> . . . Career pressures require them to support a winner, if this is at all possible. Survival within a political party is contingent upon one's proximity to those centers of political power which dispense patronage and other political favors. Remaining in opposition to a successful candidate of one's own party for too long can be disastrous to a political career. . . . Some politicians are prone to seeing everyone as subject to comparable influence. . . . However, the general public's involvement in politics is of a different order from the politician's, so that behavior characteristic of the way many politicians react to polls is extremely rare among voters.[4]

Or, as George Gallup put it in 1944: "The bandwagon theory is one of the oldest delusions of politics. It is a time-honored custom for candidates in an election to announce that they are going to win. The misconception under which these politicians labor is that a good many people will vote for a man regardless of their convictions just to be able to say that they voted for the winner."[5]

Governor Thomas Dewey, according to all the polls and observers, was certain to win the Presidency in 1948. If this so-called "bandwagon" effect were operative, Dewey should have won by a margin larger than everyone predicted, instead of tasting defeat.

In the last three Presidential elections, the bandwagon theory is completely denied by what happened to the support for the eventual loser. The Gallup Poll showed Hubert Humphrey gaining steadily from a 15 percentage point deficit in September 1968, to a 2-point deficit (before allocating the undecideds) just a few days prior to the election. (See Table 2–4 for the Humphrey trend.)

TABLE 2-4

Humphrey Support against Nixon and Wallace *

	PERCENT
September 29	28
October 10	29
October 22	31
October 27	36
November 4	40

*Report of Gallup Poll on indicated dates.

Similarly, in 1964 Goldwater, always far behind, moved from a 56-point deficit to a 29-point deficit between July and a week before election day. (See Table 2–5 for the Goldwater trend.)

TABLE 2-5

*Goldwater Support against Lyndon Johnson**

	PERCENT
July 10	20
August 23	29
September 16	29
September 27	32
October 18	29
November 2	32

*Report of Gallup Poll on indicated dates.

And, in 1960 the Nixon-Lodge ticket, beginning with a 6-point lead over Kennedy-Johnson in August, dropped steadily with the latter taking the lead in September and holding it, through the remainder of the campaign (although Nixon-Lodge almost rebounded sufficiently in the last sounding to tie the race). (See Table 2–6 for the Nixon-Lodge trend.)

Rather than being discouraged by a deficit in early trial heat figures, a campaign, like Avis, can simply try harder. In the Presidential primary in California in 1964, published polls indicated one week before the election that Nelson Rockefeller was running about ten points ahead of Barry Goldwater. Undaunted, the highly motivated Goldwater forces canvassed virtually every likely Republican household in Southern California, where Goldwater was especially strong. This rigorous effort resulted in Goldwater closing the gap and achieving a narrow victory on election day, setting him up for an impressive Convention victory. As one Rockefeller aide reflected about the poll and its impact on both camps: "First it made our California people overconfident—fat and lazy . . . and it made Goldwater's people fighting mad. They are a determined bunch once they get up a head of steam."[6]

TABLE 2-6

Nixon Support against Kennedy *

	PERCENT
August 16	50
August 30	47
September 13	47
October 11	46
October 26	45
November 7	48

*Report of Gallup Poll on indicated dates.

There is no firm evidence that poll findings—whether from leaked private surveys or from the nationally syndicated polls—directly affect the electorate. The public is impressionable in many respects, but being influenced by the polls is not one of them. Voters make up their minds for a number of reasons, most of which involve relatively straightforward calculations of self-interest. Voting for a winner in the polls is hardly a major motivating force.

"Events, not polls, affect people," writes Samuel Lubell. "Polls influence politicians most of all, and, secondly, they influence political writers, and last of all—if at all—they affect the people."[7] It is dubious that a sufficiently large proportion of the public follows the polls closely enough to get a bandwagon rolling. Those in the rank-and-file voting population who do follow the polls and remember poll results are most probably the more politically alert and active and thus those most likely to have already made up their minds and not to be so easily swayed.

Where poll results can have an impact, as we have noted, is on the flow of contributions into a campaign and the amount of attention given a candidate by the press. This can be important in the lean months when a campaign is trying to get off the ground or later on when it is attempting a final drive to bring the candidate over the top. A cycle can be set in motion: good polls, more dollars, better press coverage, and perhaps more votes. But this kind of cycle—"bandwagon"—is quite a different matter from the voter being persuaded directly by the polls that one candidate deserves his vote over another.

☞ **The Numbers Game** ☜

Leaked private polls and the results of many state polls conducted for local newspapers feed one of the entertaining diversions of American politics—the numbers game. Journalists and political observers often take hold of isolated poll findings to support their speculations of what will happen at the ballot box or to justify their explanations of what has happened.

Victory or defeat in the electoral process is no longer absolute but often becomes relative with electoral showings being judged by standards of "what was expected." Thus, it is not enough simply to win, a candidate must win big. And, to win big—even if the margin is modest or even nonexistent—is to indicate a degree of strength on election day that surpasses poll-ridden expectations. Thus, narrow victories are turned into landslides and cold defeats into moral victories.

This can happen in general election situations at any level, when the candidate is seeking to project himself as a viable candidate for a higher office. It can happen at the highest level, when the candidate for President is looking for help in getting his program through a reluctant Congress. But, it is especially rampant in primary elections. In the usual primary election situation, these divinations are construed as insights for what may happen in the general election. They reach their zenith, however, in the series of Presidential primaries that occur every four years.

One general election situation where this "insight" was manifest was in 1962 when Nelson Rockefeller ran for reelection in New York, and all understood he would seek the Presidential nomination two years later. Pundits, expecting him to win by three-quarters of a million votes, viewed his still magnificent margin of over half a million votes as disappointing and adversely affecting his Presidential prospects.

Primary election situations have two distinguishing characteristics which make projections of candidate strength from electoral showing particularly risky. One is that traditional party loyalties are not operative, and, thus, voter preferences tend to shift more frequently for more superficial reasons. A second aspect is the opportunity a primary election affords many people to vote in a protest mood, without feeling the same sense of responsibility and finality that decisions in the general election involve. For the pollster, primary races present two knotty problems. Turnout is usually considerably lower than in the general election. But also, voters in many states can vote in either party's primary contests.

In primary elections, the most dramatic evidence of the numbers game was the New Hampshire Democratic primary of 1968, which is often cited as the beginning of the end for Lyndon Johnson. Eugene McCarthy scored an impressive "victory" over the incumbent President by capturing 42 percent of the vote and almost all of New Hampshire's delegates to the Convention. Reports abounded that McCarthy's showing was testament to the unpopularity of the President's Vietnam policies and was a foretaste of the politics that would follow in the coming months.

McCarthy's "win" had little to do with the objective facts of the situation, however. Lyndon Johnson's name was not on the ballot. McCarthy was opposed by John G. Crommelin, Jacob J. Gordon, and Richard E. Lee, who together received a total of only 433 votes—or less than one percent of the vote cast. The real winner was the President, who received 50 percent of the votes. His supporters were people who had taken the time and trouble to write in his name on the ballot.

The other element of the Minnesota Senator's supposed upset was that his showing evidenced public displeasure with the Vietnam war. However, this conclusion was equally spurious. A comprehensive survey by the Survey Research Center at the University of Michigan later showed that three out of five of the people who voted for McCarthy believed the Johnson Administration's policies in Southeast Asia were not "hawkish" enough.[8]

This episode indicates the ease with which erroneous interpretations can find their way into political discourse. It was an important event, nonetheless, setting McCarthy's bandwagon in motion. We recall the 1968 primary because it evidences the eagerness with which politicians and political observers project the trends and elaborate the hidden dimensions of political behavior.

New Hampshire provided a rerun of this phenomenon in 1972 in the supposed "defeat" of Edmund Muskie. Self-appointed judges, of what should be considered an adequate showing, assumed that the Maine Senator had to obtain at least 50 percent of the Democratic vote in New Hampshire's primary, if he were to demonstrate his invulnerability in his own backyard. A poll, taken by the Becker Research Corporation for the *Boston Globe* in the Granite State in January 1972, showed

Muskie running strong with 65 percent against his challengers. From that moment on, Muskie was running against a "phantom" —as he readily acknowledged to the voters in appeals for help in getting over the 50 percent mark in the balloting—even though there were four other candidates on the ballot.

As reported in *The New York Times* on February 14, 1972, "Maria Carrier, Mr. Muskie's local coordinator, talks nervously about how hard it will be for the Maine Senator to reach 50 percent, and Mr. Muskie himself speaks resentfully about 'people who pull numbers from the air.' It is an old game, but it is being played here with unusual intensity, and it puts the news media in the position of arbiters. It is they who are asked to decide, in advance, what percentages would constitute a 'real win' for Mr. Muskie."

And then in late February another poll by the *Boston Globe* showed that Muskie's strength had dropped to 42 percent. Thus, the fact that the Senator did end up winning the primary with 48 percent of the vote appears to be of little consequence. He did poorly when he should have done well—so the conjecture went. Consider, for example, the following editorial from *The Evening Star* in Washington the day after the primary:

In such a setting, Senator Muskie hoped to take, and should have taken, more than 48% of the Democratic vote that he managed to garner. He was well known to his neighbors, apparently well-liked, and he went into New Hampshire projecting the image of an over-whelming front-runner. Now that image is smudged. His quarrel with running against a "phantom" percentage expectation is unconvincing; it would ring truer, at least, if he had made the point weeks ago when the polls were showing he had more than 60% support among New Hampshire's Democratic voters. Expectation, image and appearance are very much part of political reality.[9]

One wonders whether Muskie's national campaign for the nomination would have lost its momentum had the *Boston Globe* polls never been taken? Or was the root of the problem in the way the Senator and his staff let the reality of these poll findings haunt them rather than place them in context? Muskie, the best known of the candidates on the ballot, was bound to lose some support as the voters learned more about his challengers. It could have been pointed out to the voters that the early 65 percent showing was probably inflated for this reason.

This episode is to be contrasted to the situation in West Virginia in 1960 when John F. Kennedy took the initiative in creating his own "phantom." By obtaining over 60 percent of the vote he turned a routine victory into an apparent upset. He had told reporters on election eve that he would be "lucky to get 40 percent of the vote" in the two-way race with Hubert Humphrey, just after his own private polls showed him with a comfortable lead.[10]

☞ The Possible Political Exploitation of Survey Procedures ☜

The exploitation of the product—survey data—is one thing. There is also the potential for exploitations of procedures to affect the product. It is important and should become common practice that relevant information regarding research procedures be disclosed in reports of poll findings. However, there are some items which, if revealed in advance, could lead to the direct intervention into the research process, thus subverting its integrity and results.

During the preconvention days of 1968, both camps of the two announced Republican contenders, Richard Nixon and Nelson Rockefeller, knew well in advance when the interviews for the final preconvention Gallup Poll were to take place—July 20–23. Several days earlier, the newspapers and television were replete with the news of the sickbed endorsement of Nixon by former President Eisenhower. A sequence of five polls through July suggests that this endorsement was responsible for a sudden increase of five percentage points in Nixon's strength as against Humphrey and seven points as against McCarthy. After the Nixon peak was reached during the July 20–23 Gallup interviewing and by the time of the GOP Convention, Nixon dropped off four points as against Humphrey and six points as against McCarthy. (See Table 2–7.) The result was a temporary, but timely, explosion of the generally held belief that Rockefeller would run stronger against Humphrey and McCarthy than Nixon.

TABLE 2-7

Nixon Strength as against Humphrey and McCarthy during 1968 Preconvention Period

POLL	INTERVIEWING DATE	PERCENT FOR NIXON AS AGAINST HUMPHREY	PERCENT FOR NIXON AS AGAINST McCARTHY
Gallup	June 29-July 3	35	36
Harris	July 8-14	35	34
	Eisenhower Endorsement (July 18-19)		
Gallup	July 20-23	40	41
Crossley	July 21-26	39	37
Harris	July 25-29	36	35

A less dramatic attempt to influence poll results occurred in mid-February 1972. On the assumption that the Gallup Poll would be interviewing on the weekend of February 19 and 20, the campaign staff of Senator Humphrey spent a goodly sum for ten minutes of evening television time Thursday, February 17. Humphrey's standing in the Gallup Poll that was subsequently reported did improve slightly, but it would be hard to credit the television appearance with the achievement. Ironically, the interview dates the Humphrey staffers had counted on were incorrect and the interviews did not take place until the following weekend, February 26 and 27. Even had the interviews taken place as anticipated, it would be hard to conceive of these few minutes of television time having the impact of the Eisenhower endorsement of Richard Nixon.

Another frequently recurring type of disclosure has to do with providing advance information about political polls that are about to be reported in the press. This happens at the highest levels, and at the Presidential level it occurs regardless of whether the incumbent is a Democrat or Republican. Since the unabashed use of polls by President Kennedy has made the polls' political use respectable, White House staffers, in hot pursuit of prepublished survey data, cause their fingers to bleed and their knuckles to turn white dialing polling organizations for advance information on the President's popularity and, nearer election time, the trial heat figures. This not only endears the staffer who returns from the hunt with these morsels to his chief, it may also enable an extremely favorable White House news story to be timed coincidentally with the release by Harris or Gallup of unfavorable poll results.

While the intrinsic value of this information is marginal, it seems only fair that the party out of power should have an equal chance to get hold of it. Ambrose Bierce's sardonic definition of the "opposition" is refreshing: "In politics the party that prevents the government from running amuck by hamstringing it."[11] Ideally, of course, none of these data would be provided in advance to anyone—especially anyone in high places.

While it may seem preposterous to suggest that there is ever the possibility, it is conceivable that some political operative could obtain from a research firm of questionable competence the interviewing areas in which interviews are about to be conducted. He could then saturate local newspapers and air waves with promotional material in the hope of biasing the results of the pending survey. Thus, a favorable picture might emerge in the survey when it did not in fact exist.

This probably has never happened and, hopefully, never will. One of the most valuable things a competent opinion research firm possesses is its sample with its specification of interviewing areas. But, such recklessness is within the realm of possibility.

Another area of concern has to do with two aspects of the uses to which poll results are put. The first is the problem of the candidate who may tailor his views on substantive issues to what the polls show. The second has to do with the marketing of candidates by political-media consulting firms.

Regarding a candidate's adhering to poll results, there are three alternatives the politician has when he finds his view on an issue differs from the burden of public opinion. He can persist and try to persuade the public to his view; he can side-step the issue; or he can follow the public consensus. Each alternative can be perfectly legitimate under specific circumstances, and judgment cannot be made in any absolute terms.

We are reminded, however, of Senator Thruston Morton's recounting of how a precampaign survey indicated that the people of Kentucky thought quite highly of his record, except for his opposition to the adoption of the medicare program. He pointed out that he did not reverse himself as a result of the poll. Instead, he spelled out his reasons for opposing medicare in every speech he made in Kentucky until the election in 1962. He not only won that year, but he won by a larger margin than in the earlier 1956 race.

Regarding the marketing of candidates, the technology of the media is imposing. Segments of the electorate are singled out for specialized media appeals; television spots can allegedly correct candidate image deficiencies; and computerized direct mail campaigns can be targeted to specific voters.

At one point, an annoyed Adlai Stevenson complained: "The idea that you can merchandise candidates for high office like breakfast cereal is the ultimate indignity to the democratic process."[12] Or, as it was put by Edward Ney, President of Young and Rubicam, which handled the 1952 Eisenhower campaign and Mayor Lindsay's 1969 reelection campaign:

The propriety of using our skills to influence people in this critically important area is increasingy suspect, as, indeed, is the whole practice of selling a candidate for any political office with the same rules that one might use when promoting a product. . . . It is possible to spell out accurately the principal or marginal benefits of a chewing gum in 30 seconds. But it is virtually impossible to do necessary justice to the background, character and programs of a political candidate in the same time.[13]

Young and Rubicam has since renounced all political accounts in connection with the 1972 campaigns.

We are not competent to pass judgment on all aspects of these media politics. Suffice it to say that the technology that has been introduced into the political process cannot be held inherently "wrong" in and of itself. However, since the polling technique arrived on the scene long before the media politics, the researcher cannot but worry about the pernicious influences that may be at work in a given campaign—that the tool at which he is expert will not be used as much to elucidate public sentiment as to manipulate public passion.

While the pollster cannot be held accountable in a literal sense for the uses made of the information he turns in—either by the candidate or the political consultant—he must be alert to the ends for which his services have been solicited.

Notes

1. Quoted in *Newsday,* Weekly Magazine for Long Island, February 17, 1968, p. 30.

2. As quoted in *Time Magazine,* May 31, 1968, p. 19.

3. Leo Katcher, *Earl Warren: A Political Biography* (New York: McGraw-Hill, 1967), p. 289. This episode was also referred to by John D. Weaver in *Warren, the Man, the Court, the Era* (Boston: Little, Brown, 1967), p. 182: "They (Warren's supporters) felt they had been stabbed in the back earlier in the year when Nixon had polled some twenty-three thousand of his 1950 precinct workers, asking them to name 'the strongest candidate the Republicans could nominate for President.' One of Warren's campaign managers had flown to Washington and persuaded the Senator not to release the results, but word had already leaked out that Warren had trailed Eisenhower." For a less hostile account see Earl Mazo and Stephen Hess, *Nixon: A Political Portrait* (New York: Harper and Row, 1968), pp. 82–92.

4. Harold Mendelsohn and Irving Crespi, *Polls, Television and the New Politics* (Scranton: Chandler Publishing Co., 1970), p. 165.

5. George Gallup, *A Guide to Public Opinion Polls,* 2nd ed. (Princeton: Princeton University Press, 1948), p. 92.

6. *Newsday,* p. 30.

7. *Santa Barbara News-Press,* May 9, 1968.

8. For an excellent analysis of this period, see Richard M. Scammon and Ben J. Wattenberg, *The Real Majority* (New York: Coward-McCann, 1970), pp. 85–91.

9. *Washington Evening Star,* March 8, 1972.

10. See John M. Fenton, "The Polls—1964," *University: A Princeton Magazine,* Fall 1964.

11. Ambrose Bierce, *The Devil's Dictionary* (New York: Dover Publications, 1958), p. 94.

12. As quoted in Vance Packard, *The Hidden Persuaders* (New York: Pocket Book Edition, 1957), p. 172.

13. As quoted in Paul A. Porter, "Did You Know Ronald Reagan Shot Lincoln?", *The Washington Post,* January 23, 1972, p. 1.

3

Meaningful Uses of Polls in Politics

In no other peacetime pursuits is the need for reconnaissance so great as in love and in politics.

DR. HENRY DURANT,
British poll-taker

WHEN an individual contests for public office at the higher levels he is more than likely engaged in a once-in-a-lifetime opportunity. He is either standing for election to an office that has long been esteemed and sought, or he is running for a lesser office as the stepping-stone to greater political opportunity. At this point, why fail to take advantage of every fair means of presenting the strongest candidacy? In contrast to the misuses of the polls recounted in the previous chapter, imaginatively conceived and skillfully executed opinion polls can provide the cutting edge—especially when the opponent probably also has the advantage of polling information coming in to him.

Polls are now an essential. The candidate who usually prevails is the one who most effectively responds to the concerns of the people, and there is no better way to learn of these concerns than through opinion research. Polls can also help the candidate learn what segments of the population need to be reached out for.

Candidates are inundated with information and advice. Political lieutenants, confidants, club-house politicians, and political commentators all have their own judgments of what the mood of the people is, what the issues are, etc. But often the candidate can be seriously misled by well-intentioned supporters who whisper erroneous hints: campaigning too closely to a given individual could be dangerous; the candidate's record on an issue will hurt and, thus, should be avoided; particular segments of the electorate can be counted on only if a coalition can be created; endorsements of other public figures or advocates for special points of view are essential; etc. Without the benefit of a scientifically conducted poll, the candidate is equally often at a loss where to turn. Thus, one of the most important practical uses of the political poll is to put these kinds of counsel into perspective and to provide an "objective" check on the hunches of even the most loyal supporters.

This use of the polls is a matter quite different from the characterization by George McGovern. The night of the Ohio Presidential primary, he was seen on nationwide TV defining the difference between the old politics and the new politics as the same as the difference between "telling people what the public opinion polls say is safe and actually doing what is right for the country."

☞ The Concerns of the People ☜

"Senator Taft had never believed in polls prior to his celebrated 1950 reelection campaign for the Senate from Ohio," recalls L. Richard Guylay, who handled public relations for the late Senator's campaign. "One day at a strategy meeting of his advisers at his home in Cincinnati, he went around the table asking each in turn to give what he thought would be the principal issue of the campaign. Everyone there had a different answer. Obviously, all couldn't be right and maybe none of them was right. I said that much when it came my turn and then I added, why don't we take a poll and find out what the voters think. He told me to go ahead."[1]

Seven decades earlier, a fellow Buckeye had faced the same issue. In 1878, two years before his election as President, James Garfield remarked: "Real political issues cannot be manufactured by the leaders of political parties. The real political issues of the day declare themselves, and come out of the depths of that deep—which we call public opinion."[2]

In the days of the razzle-dazzle that makes up much of "the new politics," there is cause for concern that politicians may cynically assume that the public is impressionable enough to be whipped into a lather about almost any issue by the new political communications technologies. This, in our view, is a relatively naïve assumption, for the well-spring of a political issue is to be found in the basic concerns of the people.

In recent years, the telling political issues have come *up* from the people, not *down* from the politician—Vietnam, law and order, the cost of living, etc. Thus, it was that in 1970 candidates quickly jumped aboard the law and order issue—not only the Vice President but also good "liberals" like Adlai Stevenson, III.

Probably no other kind of data are more important to a candidate than those that portray the concerns of the people. The candidate that effectively addresses these concerns is the most likely winner. All the secondary types of poll data, such as trial heats and candidate recognition, will follow an upward trend if a candidate has managed to tie in effectively to the public's view of what the issues of real salience are. Clearly, the candidate must articulate the issues, bringing to bear information and perspectives not found among the public at large. But his posture must basically be one that comes to grips with what is on the people's minds.

Illustrative of a response to public concern was Governor Rockefeller's treatment of the issue of crime and narcotics in

41

the 1966 political season. A survey conducted in New York State showed that two of the most salient concerns of voters throughout the state were crime and narcotics. Table 3–1 shows the priority of concerns among a list of problems respondents were presented on a card. The twin problems cropped up particularly in the minds of people living in New York City.

TABLE 3-1

Public's View of Problems Facing New York State, 1966

	PERCENT MENTIONING IN:		
	STATEWIDE	NEW YORK CITY	SUBURBS & UPSTATE
Providing for state and local needs to education	23	25	21
Combating crime and juvenile delinquency	22	26	19
Dealing with the problem of narcotic addicts who take dope	9	11	7
Providing adequate state care for the mentally ill and retarded	9	8	10
Attracting industry and promoting economic growth	8	9	7
Cleaning up our rivers to reduce water pollution	6	2	10
Providing a sound program of State Medicaid for lower income families to pay their medical bills	6	3	9
Handling the problem of minimum wage level in New York State	6	5	6
Protecting consumers and the buying public	5	5	5
Keeping corruption out of the state government	4	3	5
Reducing the influence of the political bosses	3	2	3
Providing a better system of roads and expressways	1	*	2

*Less than one percent.

When respondents were asked whether they would be "more likely" or "less likely" to vote for a candidate advocating various positions on state issues, the crime issue emerged as the most telling one. (See Table 3–2) A candidate urging the "development of an all-out program to combat crime and juvenile delinquency" would be more likely to garner support than a

TABLE 3-2

Appeal of Various Stands a Candidate Could Take, 1966

	PERCENTAGE SAYING THEY WOULD BE "MORE LIKELY" TO SUPPORT A CANDIDATE MAKING EACH PROPOSAL EXCEEDS THE PERCENTAGE SAYING THEY WOULD BE "LESS LIKELY" TO SUPPORT HIM BY:		
	STATEWIDE	NEW YORK CITY	SUBURBS & UPSTATE
Development of all-out programs to combat crime and juvenile delinquency	+84 pts.	+89 pts.	+82 pts.
Spending more state money to expand and improve the care of the mentally ill and retarded	+77	+82	+71
An extensive program to clean up the state's rivers and reduce water pollution	+69	+61	+78
A proposal that narcotic addicts be hospitalized for treatment even against their will	+66	+71	+62
Spending state money to help more students in New York State attend the public or private college of their choice	+61	+72	+51
Spending over one billion dollars a year on state aid to local communities for schools	+49	+64	+34
Strong support for the Medicaid program under which New York State helps pay the medical bills of lower income families	+40	+53	+28
Spending state money to provide a better system of roads and expressways	+35	+36	+34
Strong support of equal rights and opportunities in jobs and housing for Negroes and Puerto Ricans	+34	+45	+23
Strong opposition to off-track betting	−3	−13	+5

candidate advocating any other position tested—including issues many political advisers would probably put forth as key in the voter's minds: equal rights in housing, support for Medicaid, aid to education. As Table 3–2 shows, closely allied to the crime issue in the public's mind was the strong appeal that could be made, particularly in New York City, for "a proposal that narcotic addicts be hospitalized for treatment even against their will." Thus, the Governor's narcotics program demonstrated to the voters his concern and action about a problem foremost on their minds. In the November election, after campaigning vigorously on this issue, the Governor carried three of New York City's five boroughs.

The success of Governor Rockefeller in heavily Democratic boroughs of the city is to be contrasted to the poor response of the nation to Vice President Agnew's pronouncements during the 1970 Congressional elections. Agnew spoke out again and again about protests and the general feeling of unrest across the country. His failure to capture the public imagination—as evidenced by disappointing Republican showings nationwide—is due primarily to the fact that he offered nothing affirmative. He was surely touching a sensitive nerve ending of the public with his rhetoric, but he pointed to nothing on the positive side that might help solve the problem.

☞ Maximizing Potential Strength ☜

Resources and time in a campaign are limited—and usually scarce. Thus, decisions about how and where a candidate spends his time can tip the balance to victory or defeat. Beyond that are a host of decisions with respect to media and promotional activities, research on campaign issues, and the like.

The polls are looked to for answers to many of these questions. Two aspects of the problem arise repeatedly in political research. The first has to do with the extent to which a candidate is known to the voters; the second has to do with attending to those areas in which there is the greatest chance of picking up electoral strength.

Much is made in political circles of the so-called "candidate recognition" scores. These follow from responses to questions asked whether people have heard or read about particular candidates. For example, as late as November 1971—just four months prior to the New Hampshire and Florida Democratic primaries—the name of Senator Henry Jackson was known by only 52 percent of the American public. This represented a marked improvement over the 29 percent who knew about him the previous April, but it remained a weak showing in contrast to Senators Kennedy, Humphrey and Muskie, who were known to the public with percentages of 95, 94 and 89, respectively.

The Gallup Poll which reported the 52 percent recognition figure for Senator Jackson pointed up the fact that the Senator was significantly less known among the less educated and the nonwhite population. This, however, was to be anticipated and told the Senator's campaign relatively little about what to do to increase his recognition other than to simply get more exposure.

Politicians tend to take these recognition scores very seriously, apparently feeling they represent an important barometer, and urge their inclusion in most political surveys. While recognition is often a real problem for the newcomer or nonincumbent, we question the utility of repeated measures of the degree to which a candidate is becoming better known to the voters. Knowledge that a candidate is not widely recognized does not help solve the problem, though areas where greater efforts need to be made may be pinpointed. As a campaign progresses, a previously little-known candidate will become more familiar to the public, particularly if he can tie into the basic concerns of the voters in a meaningful way.

In other words, candidate recognition is not important in its own right. As with trial heat figures, recognition scores have more meaning for measurement of progress already made than for insight about future strategy in a campaign.

A superb illustration of the point is the 1969 gubernatorial election in New Jersey, in which former Governor Robert Meyner started the campaign extremely well-known and well-liked in contrast to his challenger William Cahill, a Congressman virtually unknown in the state outside of his district. Throughout the campaign, Meyner had the advantage of being better known. In spite of this awareness advantage for Meyner, Cahill gained strength with the voters and by September—although still less known—held a nine percentage point lead over the former Governor. (See Table 3-3.)

TABLE 3-3

Awareness of Gubernatorial Candidates in New Jersey, 1969

| | PERCENT ABLE TO NAME CANDIDATES | | PERCENT SUPPORTING EACH CANDIDATE | |
	JULY	SEPTEMBER	JULY	SEPTEMBER
Meyner	59	79	43	37
Cahill	44	66	42	46
Meyner margin	+15 pts.	+13 pts.	+1 pt.	−9 pts.

The second aspect of maximizing potential strength is targeting a campaign on those areas where there is the greatest chance of picking up votes. For this a campaign needs to know three things. First, it must be determined which subgroups in the population are particularly favorable or opposed to the candidate or what he stands for. Second, a campaign will want to learn which voters presently favorable to the opposition are the most likely to switch to its own candidates; some political research firms have elaborate techniques to pinpoint these "switchers." Third, it is necessary to learn what the attitudinal make-up is of both present supporters and potential switchers from the opposition; involved here are both the priority of problems as viewed by voters and the division of opinion on specific issues.

Armed with this kind of information, a campaign can target its efforts. There then follows the decision of striking a balance between taking off from one's strength and galvanizing it or attacking areas of one's weakness in hopes of minimizing it.

While this is seldom an either-or kind of decision, a campaign will ultimately have to lean one way or the other.

In our judgment, the more effective course is the former. For by working in those areas where a candidate is particularly strong, a campaign can accomplish a number of objectives. It can solidify that strength, thereby ensuring the turnout of supporters on election day. Also, it can mobilize supporters into working for the candidate, ringing doorbells and the rest. We have already reported how effective the house-to-house blitz was in Goldwater's California campaign in which the last ditch effort was concentrated in the southern part of the state where he was strong.

Another example of the success of this approach is found in the Republican primary in 1962 when Ogden Reid challenged the incumbent Congressman in New York's 26th District. Polls showed Reid ahead of the incumbent in the northern portions of the district. They showed also that an inordinately large percentage of voters there were unable to choose between the two men. Despite the fact that this portion of the district was less populated than others, the Reid campaign was advised that it was more advantageous to concentrate on this region, working to get Reid better known and taking advantage of the favorable margin that existed in the hope of gaining the support of the undecideds. Thus, while this northern area represented only about 15 percent of the Republicans voting in the primary, 30 percent of Reid's victory margin came from there.

An historic example of going where the votes are not occurred in the last hours of the 1960 Presidential campaign. Richard Nixon, choosing to fulfill his pledge to carry his campaign into all fifty states, flew to Alaska to nail down its three electoral votes. While he did carry the state, one wonders whether the time would not have been better spent on a whirlwind tour in St. Louis, Chicago and Minneapolis-St. Paul—all areas in states falling into the Kennedy column election day by less than one percentage point. Precise last-minute polls in such key areas could have warned (and probably did) against the folly of flying off to Anchorage just before the closest election in the nation's history.

☞ Information on Image ☜

There is still another use of polling which can immeasurably aid the politician in formulating an effective campaign strategy. This use has to do with gathering intelligence on the public's view of officeholders or the competing candidates in a campaign.

"A political leader's successfully projected appearance of competence, concern, sincerity, his image in a word, can carry a far greater impact than his utterances," Professor Elmer Cornwell of Brown University perceptively points out. "The skillful executive," he adds, "will, thus, do all that he can to create and project a favorable image for himself, to build up and conserve what might be termed his 'image capital' " because "wise investment of this capital will pay better dividends than mere exhortation."[3]

And why is this so? Despite Oscar Wilde's injunction that "it is only the shallow people who do not judge by appearances,"[4] Cornwell finds that "the citizenry's capacity for information and argumentation is less than its capacity to absorb and respond to images projected by public figures. . . ."[5]

Midway in his term as Governor of Pennsylvania, Raymond Shafer had a survey conducted on his stewardship. The favorable aspects of his image in connection with the way he was handling his job were somewhat less in number and more vague than were the unfavorable aspects. (See Table 3–4.)

Rightly or wrongly, the people of Pennsylvania obviously were concerned about Shafer's spending policies in terms of what they felt they were getting back for their tax money. They

TABLE 3-4

Things Liked and Disliked about Governor Shafer

FAVORABLE		UNFAVORABLE	
Just like him, he's doing a good job, doing his best (general)	13%	Taxing too high, a wasteful spender	20%
He's bringing in industry, reducing unemployment	2	He breaks promises, doesn't fulfill pledges	6
He's for improving education	2	Has done little or nothing	4
Miscellaneous favorable	7	Not for little people, the working man	3
		Just don't like him (general)	3
		He's too political	2
		Miscellaneous unfavorable	7

also sensed that Shafer, in levying more taxes in a limited way on several minor items, had gone back on an impression of promises he had given before his election that he would not raise taxes as governor. Opposition Democrats lost no time in capitalizing on this.

Even with these poll results in hand, the governor sought a state income tax at the next meeting of the legislature. The mark of the man was that, overriding this information on these unfavorable aspects of his image, he followed his conscience and pursued the income tax so the dire educational and institutional needs of the Commonwealth would be met. The fact that he did not slavishly avoid the financial issue rendered the survey findings no less useful to him. With this information he could have better understanding as to why it eventually required two years of exhortation and a Democratic successor Milton Shapp to get the Shafer income tax idea enacted.

Data on candidate image can also explain suddenly appearing weaknesses (or strengths) in a candidate's standing. We referred earlier to the 1969 gubernatorial race in New Jersey. In these two months between the July and September surveys, Robert Meyner's strength dropped six percentage points, while that of his challenger, William Cahill, gained four points.

Between these surveys, the Cahill campaign centered around

charges that the former Governor's freedom to act in certain areas would be limited because of certain business relationships he had established since leaving office. Whatever may be said about charging someone holding no political office with conflicts of interest—or even potential conflicts of interest—the Cahill game plan worked. The impossibility of making favorable aspects of Cahill's image equal to or surpass the originally high level of Meyner's popularity in the short period of a campaign necessitated an alternative approach—attack. Evidence of the success of this approach is that the only significant difference in either the Meyner or Cahill image data between July and September occurred in the Meyner side where the category "has integrity, sincerity, dedication" fell from 12 to 6 percent. (See Table 3–5.) This occurred too late in the campaign for Meyner to overcome it and, combined with several other skillful campaign steps, the Cahill team went on to win a 6–4 victory.

TABLE 3-5

Things Liked about Meyner and Cahill

	JULY 1969	SEPTEMBER 1969	NET CHANGE
Meyner			
A good governor, good record, good job	18%	18%	—
Has integrity, sincerity, dedication	12	6	−6 pts.
Personable, popular, friendly, nice looking	8	11	+3
Qualified, capable, experienced	7	10	+3
Leans liberal, a Democrat	3	3	—
Kept taxes down, not a spender	2	1	−1
Leans conservative, like a Republican	2	1	−1
Strong, dynamic, a leader	2	1	−1
Just like him (in general)	2	1	−1
Miscellaneous on favorable side	1	1	—
Cahill			
Has done a good job, a good man	9	10	+1
Personable, pleasant, nice, patient	8	10	+2
Would make a good governor	7	9	+2
A family man	5	4	−1
Not like other Republicans	4	1	−3
Honest, fair	3	3	—
F.B.I. alumnus, ex-cop	2	1	−1
Young, dynamic	2	2	—
He's a Republican (favorable)	—	4	+4

☞ **Assessing the Trends** ☜

We have already noted the fluidity of election situations—particularly in primary contests where party loyalties do not come into play. Thus, keeping tabs on trends in opinion movement is an essential.

Overall trial heat figures are important in indicating fluctuation in voter loyalties, but far more important is learning about gains and losses that are occurring within segments of the population. When some major event has an impact on overall trial heat figures, it is only a look at what has happened internally that gives insight about what a campaign should do.

Referring back to the 1966 gubernatorial race in New York in which Governor Rockefeller targeted his efforts on the problems of crime and drugs in New York City, it will be recalled that he was making impressive gains in this traditional Democratic stronghold. However, in mid-October President Lyndon Johnson—then exceedingly popular—made a campaign appearance in the city on behalf of Frank O'Connor. Thereupon,

TABLE 3-6

New York City Gubernatorial Preferences, 1966

	ROCKEFELLER	O'CONNOR	ROCKEFELLER DEFICIT
September	19%	38%	−19 pts.
Early October	30	34	−4
	Johnson Appearance		
Mid-October	29	42	−13
Late October	31	38	−7
Election	39	42	−3

NOTE:
The "undecided" percentages were not allocated in this table and, therefore, percentages for both candidates are lower than the election results in which there are, of course, no undecideds.

Rockefeller suffered a setback with the margin separating him from O'Connor growing from four percentage points to thirteen points. (See Table 3–6.)

While these overall trial heat figures showed that the President's visit had slowed Rockefeller's drive, it was only by examination of where the Governor had suffered that a recovery effort could be mounted. Table 3-7 shows that the President's visit had its greatest impact among the less educated, those living in households with an income of under $4,000, and non-whites.

TABLE 3-7

New York State Gubernatorial Preferences, 1966
(among special groups)

	ROCKEFELLER	O'CONNOR	ROCKEFELLER DEFICIT
Grade School Educated			
September	17%	41%	−24 pts.
Early October	24	38	−14
Mid-October	25	49	−24
Late October	29	42	−13
Household Income under $4000			
September	21	41	−20
Early October	27	39	−12
Mid-October	25	48	−23
Late October	34	39	−5
Nonwhites			
September	17	46	−29
Early October	29	38	−9
Mid-October	21	48	−27
Late October	30	43	−13

☞ **Assessing the Impact of a Third Candidate** ☜

The survey technique can also be put to use to assess the interdependencies existing between races in a given state or between the sources of strength of candidates in the same race. Research

52

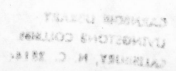

can stave off the common error of political strategists in assuming that the support for candidates of like political complexion is almost interchangeable. Thus, it might be concluded that "liberals" in the same contest detract from each other.

Much has been made of the "spoiler" role Franklin D. Roosevelt, Jr. is supposed to have played in the reelection of Nelson Rockefeller as Governor of New York in 1966. It is held by some commentators that Roosevelt's defection from the Democratic fold to stand as the Liberal Party's candidate cost O'Connor, the Democratic candidate, a sufficient number of votes to ensure Rockefeller's victory. It is pointed out that the number of votes Roosevelt won (507,234) exceeded the margin dividing Rockefeller and O'Connor (392,263). Thus, had Roosevelt not run, it is contended, his support would have been enough to put O'Connor over the top.

Surveys just prior to the November election, however, showed that for every three votes Roosevelt drew from O'Connor, he also drew one vote from Rockefeller. Thus, while Roosevelt's candidacy obviously hurt O'Connor considerably more than it did Rockefeller, it is doubtful that it kept Frank O'Connor from the governorship.

As Democratic Presidential aspirants were sorting themselves out prior to the 1972 convention, it was commonly assumed that if Senator Edward Kennedy were not a candidate, Senator Muskie would be the prime beneficiary. Not only are both men Roman Catholics and from the same section of the country, but they are regarded as having much the same kind of "liberal" appeal in contrast to Senator Humphrey, for example, who it was alleged had the legacy of Vietnam and the 1968 Chicago Convention to overcome. Yet, pundits were surprised in December 1971, when the Gallup Poll reported that if Kennedy did not run the bulk of his support among Democrats would go to Humphrey. In fact, Humphrey would gain more than twice as much as Muskie. Thus, other factors were at work in the public's mind. (See Table 3-8.)

This kind of polling information can help alert a candidate to the impact on his campaign of his party's candidate for another office in the same election. Looking to New York again, the strength of James Buckley, the Conservative Party's candidate for the Senate in 1970, presented serious problems for Nelson Rockefeller, who was up for reelection. A poll just prior to the election showed Buckley to be a very strong candidate—drawing 34 percent of the total vote and 47 percent of the vote among Republicans—against the Republican Party's candidate Charles Goodell and the Democratic candidate Richard Ottinger. The poll also showed that only 31 percent of Rockefeller's backers intended to vote for Goodell, whereas 51 percent of his supporters intended to vote for Buckley. (See Table 3-9.)

Rockefeller's opponent Arthur Goldberg had a somewhat similar problem because the Liberal Party had endorsed both

TABLE 3-8

Impact of Kennedy Candidacy on Preferences of Democrats

	WITH KENNEDY IN	WITH KENNEDY OUT	NET GAIN
Kennedy	32%	—	—
Muskie	25	31%	+6 pts.
Humphrey	19	34	+15
All others	18	27	+9
Undecided	6	8	+2

TABLE 3-9

Senate vs. Gubernatorial Voter Preferences in New York, 1970

	SENATE PREFERENCE			
	GOODELL	OTTINGER	BUCKLEY	
Rockefeller supporters	31%	18%	51%	100%
Goldberg supporters	24	64	12	100
Adams supporters	7	24	69	100

him and Goodell. Of Goldberg's supporters, about one-in-four (24 percent) intended to vote for Goodell. However, Goldberg's problem was not comparable to that faced by the Governor. Thus, when the press charged that Rockefeller was not going all out for his fellow Republican, Goodell publicly recognized that the Governor's constituency of support was considerably different from his own.

☞ **Positioning the Issue** ☜

A continuing dilemma for the candidate is finding the most appropriate context within which to address an issue—or to use Lloyd Free's phrase, "positioning the issue."[6] This assumes the candidate has made up his mind as to his own stand on an issue and is looking for the best way to present his case.

Survey research can make important contributions by trying out arguments and appeals on the public to find out which are the most effective in convincing people of the soundness of one's position.

In early 1968, for example, both sides of the Vietnam debate could have learned how best to argue their case from a survey conducted by the Institute for International Social Research. This study showed that both the Johnson Administration and the peace movement were using some of the least effective arguments in behalf of their causes.

Specifically, respondents in a national sample were shown a card on which were listed "arguments that have been given for continuing our military efforts in Vietnam." They were asked "which two or three of these do you, yourself, feel are the very strongest arguments?" As Table 3–10 portrays, two of the least effective arguments at the time were those advanced by proponents of a continued U.S. presence in Vietnam: "we are committed to South Vietnam" and "if we pull out and the com-

POLLS

munists take over, they will kill many of the Vietnamese who have opposed them."

TABLE 3-10

Strongest Arguments Selected for
Continuing Our Military Effort in Vietnam, 1968

If we do not continue, the Communists will take over Vietnam and then move on to other parts of the world	49%
We must support our fighting men	48
If we quit now, it would weaken the will of other countries to defend their freedom	33
If we give up, the whole expenditure of American lives and money will have been in vain	33
The U.S. should never accept defeat	24
If we do not continue, we will lose prestige and the confidence of our friends and allies abroad	23
We are committed to South Vietnam	19
If we pull out and the Communists take over, they will kill many of the Vietnamese who have opposed them	14
If we persevere, we are sure to gain our objectives	8

On the other side of the coin, respondents were shown another list of "arguments that have been given for our discontinuing the struggle to win the war and beginning to pull out gradually in the near future." They were again asked which two or three arguments were the strongest. Table 3–11 shows that three of the arguments used by the peace movement were, at the time, among the least effective: "our participation in the war in Vietnam is basically illegal and immoral . . . ," "our national interest and security do not require us to fight in Vietnam," and "we are doing too much damage to the Vietnamese people, their way of life and their economy."

The same technique was employed in New Jersey during the gubernatorial race of 1965. At the same time, there was much debate over the kind of tax program that should be instituted and people were divided over the relative merits of an income tax as opposed to a sales tax. A survey in June 1965 showed

56

TABLE 3-11

*Strongest Arguments Selected for
Discontinuing the Struggle to Win the War, 1968*

Too many Americans are being killed or wounded	39%
The war is dividing the American people and affecting our national unity	31
The South Vietnamese are not doing their share in the war effort	30
The people in South Vietnam are so divided and there is so little national unity that there is no foundation for a strong independent country	29
We may end up having to fight China, Russia, or both—even a nuclear war	29
Expending so much of our military strength on the war in Vietnam has weakened our ability to respond to danger in other parts of the world	22
We are wasting too much money that could be better used for other purposes	21
The chance of succeeding either by military force or through negotiations is remote	14
Most people abroad are highly critical of our actions in Vietnam	11
Our participation in the war in Vietnam is basically illegal and immoral; we have no business being there at all	9
Our national interest and security do not require us to fight in Vietnam	9
We are doing too much damage to the Vietnamese people, their way of life and their economy	9

that advocates of the unpopular income tax proposal could make their strongest case by pointing out to the public two things: that "a sales tax would make everything cost more" and that "an income tax would allow deductions for dependents, medical expenses, etc." They would be ill-advised to argue that "a sales tax would hurt business conditions" or that "if the state had an income tax, the people least able to pay could expect to pay nothing or almost nothing (in taxes)." (See Table 3–12.)

57

TABLE 3-12

*Strongest Arguments Selected for an Income Tax
Rather Than a Sales Tax in New Jersey, 1965*

A sales tax would make everything cost more (except food and drugs)	34%
A state income tax would allow deductions for dependents, medical expenses, etc.	26
A state income tax is fair to me and my family because people with more income would pay a higher tax	21
A state income tax would in the end cost me and my family less than a sales tax	18
Paying the two or three cents sales tax on each dollar spent would be a nuisance	18
The state income tax would not hurt too much because it would be paid through payroll deductions	18
A sales tax would hurt business conditions by affecting the sales volume of our merchants	14
If the state had an income tax, my family and I would expect to have to pay nothing or almost nothing	11

Conversely, proponents of a sales tax over an income tax would likely gain more supporters by arguing that a sales tax is fairest "because everyone would pay the same rate." They would likely persuade fewer by arguing that a state income tax on top of the federal income tax would be too much of a burden, that an income tax would keep industry from coming into the state, and that the amount of a sales tax paid could be controlled by a family through the device of buying less.[7] (See Table 3–13.)

☞ Targeting the Opposition's Weakness ☜

In a manner related to positioning the issue, it is possible to target the opposing candidate's areas of weakness—particularly with respect to issues that will most adversely affect his candi-

TABLE 3-13

*Strongest Arguments Selected for a Sales Tax
Rather Than an Income Tax in New Jersey, 1965*

The sales tax is fair to me and my family because everyone else would pay the same rate	39%
A sales tax is being paid partly by people from other states who buy things in this state	30
The sales tax would not hurt too much because it is paid in small amounts at a time	26
Filling out still another income tax form each year—this one for the state—would be a great nuisance to me	26
A sales tax would in the end cost me and my family less than an income tax	24
A state income tax would keep industry from locating in the state and affect jobs	22
A state income tax, on top of the federal income tax, would be too great a burden from this kind of tax	22
If the state had a sales tax, my family and I would be able to keep the total amount down by buying less	15

dacy. When an opposing candidate is clearly identified in the public's mind with a given stance on a salient issue, the task of targeting is simplified considerably. However, even when the opposition is not so clearly perceived as holding a controversial or unpopular position, the survey technique can provide useful insights as to where vulnerabilities may begin to appear.

Referring again to the New Jersey gubernatorial election of 1965, Wayne Dumont, the Republican candidate, had long been an advocate of a sales tax and had opposed any move toward a state income tax. He had also spoken out against bond issues to raise money for state projects. His opponent, the incumbent Richard Hughes, was not closely identified with any tax alternative in the view of New Jersey voters.

In the June 1965 survey respondents were asked whether the advocacy of various positions with respect to state revenues would make them "more likely to support a candidate, less likely, or wouldn't make much difference one way or the other." As Table 3–14 vividly shows, the greatest opposition among voters would be toward the candidate who advocated a state income tax. A sales tax and bond issues were not popular but were less troublesome than the income tax. What people did favor was a state lottery.

As the campaign went forth, Dumont had to overcome his past identification with the sales tax, while Governor Hughes was not burdened by any tax image at all. Hughes's relative advantage over Dumont probably contributed largely to his victory. After the election, when it became clear some revenue measure was necessary, Hughes advocated a state income tax. But failing this, he advocated and put through the less unpopular sales tax. The strong showing for the lottery pinpoints why New Jersey has one today.

TABLE 3-14

Impact of a Candidate's Advocacy of Alternative Revenue Plans in New Jersey, 1965

	HOW PROPOSAL WOULD AFFECT VOTE			
	MORE LIKELY	LESS LIKELY	MORE LIKELY MINUS LESS LIKELY	WOULDN'T MAKE MUCH DIFFERENCE
A Candidate Who—				
Favored a state lottery or sweepstakes	59%	20%	+39 pts.	10%
Favored a state sales tax	34	45	−11	9
Consistently opposed state bond issues	25	41	−16	8
Favored a state income tax	21	60	−39	7

The same issue appeared in the 1964 gubernatorial race in Indiana. A survey conducted in the state in March reported that "Marshall Kizer and Thomas Lemon (two contenders for the Democratic nomination) have spoken out against the sales tax and in favor of a graduated income tax along federal tax lines. Only 17 percent of likely November voters who favored these candidates over Lieutenant Governor Richard Ristine (the Republican candidate) agreed with them in this position: over two-thirds of those who supported Kizer or Lemon over Ristine preferred one of the other tax alternatives."[8]

Whether the Democrats had information of this kind is not known. However, their decision to overlook Kizer and Lemon in favor of Roger Branigin, who was not identified by the voters with any particular tax position, was a shrewd one, for Branigin went on to defeat the conscientious Ristine, who was remembered by the public as breaking a tie vote in the State Senate to bring about a tax program combining a moderate sales and income tax.

No candidate in recent years has been so clearly pegged by voters with his stand on substantive issues as Barry Goldwater. The unpopularity of his stand on many issues was ultimately to be his undoing nationally in 1964. A foretaste of this came in the New Hampshire primary in 1964 when Governor Rockefeller outlined in detail to voters the Senator's stand on issues. A survey of Republicans in the Granite State three months prior to the primary reported that those voters supporting Goldwater over Rockefeller overwhelmingly opposed the Senator's stand (or at least his written position) on a host of issues:

66% opposed withdrawal from the United Nations if Communist China was admitted;

88% opposed breaking diplomatic relations with Russia;

68% approved of the Nuclear Test Ban Treaty;

80% opposed putting Social Security on a voluntary basis;

76% favored the graduated income tax;

70% favored Federal grants to the states to help those needing welfare aid;

62% favored Federal aid to education for school and college construction and loans to college students;

57% favored the inclusion of a public accommodations provision in a civil rights bill;

83% favored the fixing of minimum wages by the Federal Government.

61

While Rockefeller did not win in New Hampshire, he certainly did soften up the support that eventually went to Henry Cabot Lodge.

These instances are those in which candidates were especially identified with particular postures on central issues. What of the case in which a politician is not so identified? Surveys can indicate the weak links in the opposition's argument which may, at a later date, prove to be salient enough with the public to target efforts toward.

TABLE 3-15

Strongest Arguments against
Economic Policies of Nixon Administration

The freeze on wages and prices is not fair to the working man because business profits and dividends are not also included	34%
President Nixon is proposing too large a tax reduction for business and not enough for the working man, and this is not fair	34
The freeze on wages and prices is not likely to hold down the rising cost of living	25
President Nixon is more concerned about controlling the rising cost of living than he is about the rising rate of unemployment	20
By raising duties on products imported from other countries, the U.S. is risking an international trade war and is raising the cost of imported products for Americans	18
President Nixon has not listened closely enough to representatives of business, labor, and the public in formulating this new economic program	12
The program has undermined worldwide confidence in the American dollar	11

Illustrative of this use of a political survey was the interest of the Democratic National Committee in learning how best to respond to the economic policies President Nixon announced in the Fall of 1971. A study was commissioned in which people were given a card listing seven arguments against the wage and price control policies just announced by the President. They were asked which one or two of the arguments they felt were most compelling.

It was learned that of all the attacks that could be mounted on the President's economic program, none evidenced greater public support than the issue of the equity of the controls. As Table 3–15 indicates, there was little concern among the people over the international ramifications of controls. There was also little response to the argument that the President had not listened closely enough to representatives of business, labor, and the public.[9]

These, then, are some of the practical uses to which polls are put in politics. With this as background we now turn to some of the considerations the layman should keep in mind when reading and using polls. We will look first at the question of why polls are reliable at all—why interviews with only 1,500 people can possibly be expected to represent faithfully the views of the entire nation. We will then highlight some of the factors to be considered when interpreting political polls.

Notes

1. Letter to Charles W. Roll, Jr., January 20, 1972.
2. Speech in Boston, Mass., September 10, 1878, as quoted in *A New Dictionary of Quotations,* ed. H. L. Mencken (New York: A. A. Knopf, 1942), p. 874.
3. Elmer E. Cornwell, Jr., "Role of the Press in Presidential Politics" in *Politics and the Press,* ed. Richard W. Lee (Washington: Acropolis Books, 1970), p. 19.
4. Quoted in *The Wit and Humor of Oscar Wilde,* ed. Alvin Redman (New York: Dover Publications, 1959), p. 137
5. Cornwell, "Role of the Press in Presidential Politics," p. 19.

6. In conversations with the authors.

7. These reasons were designed by Archibald M. Crossley.

8. Unpublished survey report, April, 1964.

9. Center for Political Research, *National Journal* 3, no. 52 (December 25, 1971): 2,548.

Why Is a Poll Reliable?

Probability is the very guide of life.
BISHOP JOSEPH BUTLER

HOW can interviews with only 1,500 people possibly provide a faithful portrait of a nation at large? Why do 1,500 interviews give you virtually the same precision regardless of how large a population is being surveyed? Why do interviews obtained in one state as part of a national survey not represent a good sample of that state? Why do people who fall into an opinion sample not have to be representative of anything in particular? How can you tell how good a sample is?

These questions are often asked. They reflect the air of mystery and misunderstanding surrounding the process of sampling—the immense unseen foundation of an opinion poll. Of all the procedures involved in polling, none is more critical to the quality of the product. It is for this reason we devote a chapter to sampling—the theory and the practice.

☞ Different Ways a Sample Can Be Drawn ☜

There are three basic types of samples that have been used in survey research: purposive, quota, and probability. Each has its advantages and disadvantages.

65

POLLS

PURPOSIVE SAMPLING

In 1959, the Gallup Poll was interested in undertaking a survey to find out what factors might contribute to long life. It was decided to draw a sample of people 95 years of age or older. But people qualifying for this kind of a sample could not easily be found among the population because of their rarity. Therefore, they were sought out in those places where they could be found in groups, such as old soldiers' homes, nursing homes, etc.[1] For the needs of the study, this kind of sampling procedure was adequate, and, in fact, may have been the only practical way to do it.

QUOTA SAMPLING

Whenever possible, however, some more careful basis is required for determining who is to be interviewed. One of the earliest procedures adopted in surveys was quota sampling. In this type of sampling, census data are consulted to find the distribution of the population by characteristics such as sex, age, region, and economic well-being. An overall framework is designed so that the distribution of interviews within the sample will match the census distribution. Interviewers are given assignments in which respondents are allocated according to quotas of specific characteristics (so many men, so many women; so many under 30 years of age, so many between 31 and 45 years, so many 46 years or older; etc.). The choice of the people actually interviewed is then left up to the interviewer.

The principal attraction of quota sampling is that it is comparatively economical. Since interviewers are not obligated to go to a specified block area, they do not need to be compensated for the time frequently required to obtain the interviews assigned in a designated area. This reduces the cost.

Quota sampling has several drawbacks, however, which have discouraged many opinion research firms from relying upon

66

it. The most important is that since the interviewer's judgment intervenes in determining which individual is to be interviewed, the element of randomness is lost. As a result, the theory of probability does not apply, and it is not possible to calculate the chance that the sample is a fluke and not representative of the population being surveyed.

A second drawback is that the interviewer may not obtain a representative group of respondents within the quotas. He may inadvertently over- or underrepresent individuals of a particular type. Thus, he might, for example, fill his quota of people 65 years of age and older with only 65 and 66 year olds, so that others in this quota are underrepresented.[2]

Quota sampling fell into disrepute in 1948 when it served as the basis for predictions that Dewey would defeat Truman. It was held accountable again in Britain in 1970 when many polls predicted the defeat of Edward Heath's Conservative Party.

PROBABILITY SAMPLING

Most opinion research firms now rely upon probability principles in one way or another in drawing their samples. The essential notion in this type of sampling procedure, if carried out fully, is that every individual has an equal or known chance of falling into the sample.

The most common procedure is to divide the overall population into separate categories (or "strata") according to the size of the locality the people live in. Specific geographic areas are then determined on a systematic (or on a random) basis in which a specified number of interviews are to be conducted.[3] The people actually interviewed fall into the sample on a chance basis. They are not interviewed because they are representative of any particular population characteristic. Rather, they are interviewed solely because the area in which they live has fallen into the sample.

Probability sampling procedures are generally regarded as

the preferred procedures. They result in the closest approximation of *all* characteristics of the population being surveyed—not just those characteristics the census reports data about, but all characteristics. Thus, by this method cigarette smokers, registered Republicans, and regular churchgoers, for example, should fall into the sample with a degree of precision that can be predicted from probability theory—even though the Census does not report these kinds of data.

☞ The Theory behind Probability Sampling ☜

If probability procedures are strictly followed, the odds are that the sample will be a faithful representation of the population. But why should this be so? The simplest explanation is found in the following illustration. Suppose one had a large barrel containing 10,000 marbles, 5,000 of which were red and 5,000 green, and wanted to draw a probability sample of 400 marbles. Blindfolded, one would draw the first marble. To insure that all the remaining marbles had an equal chance of being drawn, the barrel would be shaken after each subsequent drawing until the 400 marbles had been drawn.

Conceivably, the sample drawn could consist of one red marble and 399 green (or vice versa). It is more likely, however, that it would be fairly close to the 50–50 division actually existing in the barrel of 10,000—that is, approximately 200 red marbles and 200 green.

If one were to repeat this procedure 100, 1,000, or an infinite number of times, the laws of probability tell us that the most frequently drawn combination we can expect in the sample of 400 marbles is 200 red and 200 green. The next most frequently drawn combination would be either 199 red and 201 green, or

199 green and 201 red, then either 198 red and 202 green, or vice versa, and so on down to the extremely rare draw of 400 of one color alone.

It is the same with an opinion survey. An infinite number of samples can be drawn of a given population. If each individual in the population being surveyed has an equal or known chance of falling into the sample, the odds are large that the sample will end up being sufficiently representative to provide accurate data, just as the odds are large that a representative number of red and green marbles will be drawn from the barrel—or at least a nearly equal (or sufficiently representative) number will fall into the sample of marbles drawn.

THE CONCEPT OF SAMPLING ERROR

Through statistics, it is possible to calculate exactly what the chances are that the sample drawn is representative of the population; i.e., the chances the sample is not one of the exceedingly unlikely fluke samples from among the infinite number of samples that could possibly be drawn.

"Sampling error" is the term used to describe the degree to which the results obtained in a single sampling can be expected to vary from the results that would be obtained if an infinite number of samples of people were interviewed. Or, to put it another way, sampling error is the degree to which the results in a sample can be expected to differ from the results that would emerge if everyone in the population had been interviewed.

Sampling error in a survey is not error caused by inexact answers to poorly worded questions, by sloppy sampling procedures or by any other type of human fallibility. It is, rather, the result of the fact that an element of chance enters when one is dealing with randomly drawn samples.

Sampling error can be expressed in terms of a range (numbers of percentage points) above and below a reported percentage within which the results of an infinite number of samplings would fall.

The size of the margin of error to be considered in a given survey situation can depend upon the "level of confidence" in the survey desired. The standard is the 95-confidence level. This means that in an infinite number of similarly designed and conducted surveys, the percentages would fall within a given margin of error in 95 percent of these surveys. This is the standard level of confidence applied to all sample surveys. Theoretically, if we wanted to increase the confidence level to 99 percent of an infinite number of surveys, the margin of error would have to be increased by about 30 percent. If we were satisfied with a confidence level of 68 percent, we could reduce the expected margin by half.

Taking a specific example, on the eve of the 1968 Presidential election, the Gallup Poll reported that 43 percent of the vote cast for President would go to Richard Nixon, 42 percent would go to Hubert Humphrey, and the remaining 15 percent would go to George Wallace. Based upon the number of interviews obtained in that final preelection survey, the laws of probability tell us that in 95 out of 100 samplings in an infinite series of similarly-drawn samples, the margin of error would be 2 percentage points. That is, the Nixon percentage could be expected to be no less than 41 percent and no more than 45 percent, with the most likely percentage expected to be 43 percent. Similarly, the Humphrey percentage could be expected to be no less than 40 percent and no more than 44 percent, with the most likely percentage being 42 percent.

The laws of probability also indicate, however, that there was a better than even chance—68 chances out of 100—that both the Nixon and Humphrey percentages could be expected to be within one percentage point of the survey results (one-half the expected error for the 95 percent level of confidence).

70

So, to fall within expected sampling error range is testimony to the quality of the sample that was drawn. However, to go the next step and come up with the winner in as close a race as this one is in large portion luck. Election eve developments can affect returns in unpredictable ways. And, it is possible that in a close race a poll can point to the wrong winner even though its results are well within the boundaries of probable sampling error. It is for these, among other reasons, that election eve polls should not be read as "predictions." Things being what they are, the major national polls are bound to err again as they did in 1948. Much derision will follow as the experts are made "fools" of again.

The point needs to be restated that what election eve polls represent is the reading of public opinion the week prior to the election. They cannot be held up to the polling community as outright predictions. It is for this reason that a poll should not be judged by whether or not it "picks" the winner. The only valid measure is whether the election results fall within the range that must be allowed to account for sampling error— assuming that no world-shaking events have transpired in the last hours of the campaign.

If one deals at the 95 percent level of confidence, it is theoretically possible that 5 percent of the samples could vary beyond the margin of error allowed for. Thus, in the case of the 1968 election, was there not a 5 percent chance the poll results could have been 3 or more percentage points off—perhaps even 10 or more percentage points off? In most polls this would be theoretically possible.

WHAT SAMPLING ERROR DEPENDS UPON

In a probability sample, sampling error is largely determined by the size of the sample, *not* the size of the overall population being surveyed.[4] The larger the sample, the smaller the sampling error that can be expected. A kind of law of diminishing returns applies, however, such that each additional person included in the sample adds less and less to reducing sample error.

Table 4–1 shows the expected sampling error for samples of different size based upon procedures presently used by the Gallup Poll.

TABLE 4-1

Sample Size and Sampling Error*

NUMBER OF INTERVIEWS	MARGIN OF ERROR (IN PERCENTAGE POINTS)
4,000	±2
1,500	±3
1,000	±4
750	±4
600	±5
400	±6
200	±8
100	±11

*Based upon sampling error as calculated from experience with the Gallup sample.

Thus, suppose a survey based on 1,500 interviews showed President Nixon drawing support from 50 percent of the population. He might actually be supported by as few as 47 percent or as many as 53 percent, with the most likely being the 50 percent turned up in the survey. At the other extreme, if the 50 percent support for Nixon were based upon a sample of only 100 interviews, the actual degree of support might be as low as 39 percent or as high as 61 percent, with the most likely again being the 50 percent obtained.

Determining the sample size to be employed in a survey involves achieving a balance between considerations of the precision needed and the cost of the survey. Obviously, the more interviews that are conducted, the greater the cost. (The cost of most surveys is usually figured on a cost per interview basis.)

Thus, would it be worth nearly doubling the cost of a survey by increasing the sample size from 750 to 1,500 in order to reduce the expected sampling error from plus or minus 4 percentage points to plus or minus 3 percentage points?

In two instances it can be well worth the cost of increasing sample size. The first is in election eve measurements. Obviously, one wants to achieve the smallest expected sampling error within reasonable limits. Thus, a larger sample is required not only to reduce the sampling error, but also to allow for eliminating the unlikely voters. In contrast to this kind of survey is one in which the focus is on many opinion questions for which the same degree of precision is not required. For example, there are questions about many issues in which it is only the general division of opinion that is being measured, or there are candidate image questions which measure only generalized impressions of candidates. It does not make much real difference whether 65 percent favor "no fault" auto insurance or 59 percent or 71 percent.

A second instance in which larger sample sizes are appropriate is when differences within groups in the sample might be important, e.g., differences between age groups, regions of the areas being surveyed, partisan loyalties, etc. If it were crucial to a study to determine how the views of women differed from men, for example, the sample would need to be doubled since only one-half of the interviews obtained would be with women.

As we noted earlier, sampling error depends upon the size of the sample. This rule applies, however, only when a sample is drawn along probability lines. The huge sample sizes of the straw polls give a seductive impression of precision. The fabled *Literary Digest* mailed out ten million questionnaires and based its prediction in 1936 upon the two million questionnaires that were returned. However, the effort was fruitless since the returned questionnaires had nothing to do with a probability sample. Thus, it is not surprising that the *Digest*'s prediction erred by about 20 percentage points when it claimed Roosevelt would lose with only 40.9 percent of the vote.

Similar miscalls occurred in the straw polls of the *New York Daily News* on three separate occasions when about 30,000 so-called straws were collected each time. On 1938's election eve the *News* said, "Thomas E. Dewey will be the next Governor of New York State" but Herbert Lehman was reelected. In 1944, New York State's civilian vote for President was supposed to be carried by Dewey—it actually went to F.D.R. by nearly four points. And in 1966, the *News* proclamation that "Democrat Frank D. O'Connor will be elected Governor of New York tomorrow . . . in a very tight race" proved to be wildly in error when Rockefeller won by over six percentage points.[5]

Therefore, the key factor in sampling is not having a sample of massive size, but how a sample is drawn.

POPULATION SIZE AND SAMPLING ERROR

Another misconception about survey sampling is that the larger the population to be sampled, the larger the sample that is needed. This, however, is not the case, since expected sampling error depends only slightly upon the size of the population under study if it is a large population. To achieve a sampling error of plus or minus three percentage points requires a sample of 1,500 interviews—regardless of whether one is surveying a city, a state, or the nation.

While the justification for this is found in probability theory, it also follows common sense. If 1,500 interviews were conducted among the 215,401 residents of Lane County, Oregon, in which Eugene and the University of Oregon are situated, only a small portion of the total population would be interviewed. Similarly, 1,500 interviews represent an even smaller fraction of the total population of the State of Oregon (2,091,385) and an even smaller portion of the nation's population (203,-

TABLE 4-2

Samples as Proportions of Population

	POPULATION	PORTION REPRESENTED BY 1,500 INTERVIEWS
Lane County, Oregon	215,401	.0069633
The State of Oregon	2,091,385	.0007172
U.S.A.	203,184,772	.0000074

184,772). Table 4–2 shows how small these portions are.

In all cases the portion represented by the 1,500 interviews is infinitesimally small. If one were satisfied that a 1,500 case sample was sufficient to measure opinion in Lane County but urged that the sample size be increased nine or ten times for the Oregon survey, the portion of the total state population represented by the sample would still be only about .007172—still infinitesimal in comparison to the total population.

The reader will recall the earlier explanation of probability theory through the example of a barrel of marbles, half of which were red and half green. In the example, it was imagined that the barrel contained 10,000 marbles. The most probable division of marbles that would be drawn in the sample was 50–50. Imagine, however, that the barrel contained 1,000,000 marbles, half red and half green. The most probable division of the 400 marbles drawn from the barrel is still 50–50, despite the fact the total number of marbles has been increased.

It will also be recalled that the larger the sample of marbles that was drawn, the surer one could be that the 50–50 split would be reflected in the marbles drawn. Thus, the degree of confidence one has in the sample depends upon how the sample is drawn and how large it is—not the size of the population from which the sample is drawn.[6]

🖙 Interviewing Areas 🖙

Since people are not marbles in a jar, we must adapt the sampling theory to the problem of population sampling. Of course, if the names of the entire adult population were stored in one repository and kept current—with names being removed as people died and being added as teenagers become 18— theoretically we might follow the marbles-in-a-jar procedure in drawing a sample. However, even if such a repository did exist, the process might prove unwieldy.

Therefore, we must look to other methods of selecting respondents for interview. Since virtually everyone resides someplace, the drawing of samples involves the selection of interviewing areas (or sampling points) containing groups of households.[7] Therefore, people end up falling into the sample because of where they happen to live and not because of who they are or what they supposedly represent.

In each of these interviewing areas, a specific number of interviews are to be conducted. These interviewing areas are determined through random procedures. In the case of an urban area, a sampling point might be a city block or several city blocks. In the case of rural areas, sampling points are usually segments of a township or some other small subdivision. Since sampling points are drawn into the sample on a probability basis, when they are combined together the overall sample is assured of being representative of the population being surveyed.

At each sampling point, a "cluster" of interviews is obtained. It would be possible to conduct only one interview at each sampling point, but this would require interviewers to travel distances to reach the specific areas in which each separate interview was to be conducted. Costs can be reduced without sacrificing the probability aspects of the sample by selecting several hundred sampling points, in the case of a national survey, in which interviewers obtain a cluster of interviews.

THE PROBLEM OF REPRESENTATIVENESS

One of the most common misconceptions about sampling is that interviewing areas and the individuals interviewed in each area must be "typical" of that area or of the overall population. Thus continues the erroneous line of thought: a sample is representative only if its parts are representative or are made up of what are thought to be "average" Americans, New Yorkers, etc.

An interviewer who should know better will ask his employer to reassign him to an interviewing area which may be more convenient for him or in which he prefers to work. He frequently adds that the area assigned him was not "typical" anyway.

Also, it is often that one reads a newspaper columnist who complains that 1,500 interviews for the entire country means that each respondent interviewed is supposed to represent 85,-000 people.

As the foregoing discussion indicates, respondents or sampling points are *not* selected because of their typicality or of their representativeness. Rather, each sampling area and each individual falls into the sample by chance and thus contributes a certain uniqueness to the whole. It is only when these unrepresentative elements are added together that the sample should become representative.

THE IMPORTANCE OF DISPERSION

When probability sampling involves the selection of sampling points in which clusters of interviews are conducted, a determination must be made of how many sampling points are required. At one extreme would be to obtain all interviews of, say, a 1,000 case sample from one interviewing area. This is analogous to the so-called barometer approach. The danger of this approach is that the one area selected is not likely to prove representative or, if it is selected for its representativeness, it is not likely to remain representative long. Even if the 1,000 people drawn into the sample from the sole area selected include a good distribution of people by characteristics, such as age, education, income level, race, religion, etc., it would almost certainly not reflect the proper mix of people with regard to other characteristics, such as institutional and cultural influences of other regions or other types of communities.

At the other extreme would be obtaining one interview in each interviewing area. Thus, for a 1,000 case sample there would be 1,000 interviewing areas. This approach is, however, prohibitively expensive. Not only is the task of selecting interviewing areas and delineating the one household in which the single interview is to be conducted time consuming, and thus costly, but considerable time and expense is involved in dispatching the interviewer the distances required to complete the assignment.

Therefore, a balance must be struck between considerations of adequate dispersion of sampling points and cost. The number of interviews conducted in each sampling point ranges from 4 to 12. Some time back the Gallup Poll assigned 10 interviews in each of 150 sampling points to achieve its 1,500 case national samples. It now assigns clusters of 5 interviews for each of more than 300 sampling points, thus achieving greater dispersion.

General population samples that involve clusters of more than 14 or 15 personal interviews may be pushing considerations of economy to the detriment of considerations of dispersion. In a country like ours, where people of the same race and income bracket tend to live in the same neighborhoods, too many interviews in too few sampling points poses the risk of not producing the right proportions of such population characteristics. Thus, a national sample based upon 50 interviewing areas where 20 interviews are obtained in each would be somewhat less likely to yield the proper proportions with regard to race, income level, and even occupation or political party affiliation than would a sample of 200 interviewing areas with 5 interviews in each. On the other hand, in any country or survey situation where there would be a near-perfect distribution of population characteristics throughout the population (such as income level, race, etc.), the number and dispersion of interviewing areas becomes less important.

In other words, the greater the dispersion of interviewing areas—and the fewer interviews assigned per area—the more likely it is that population characteristics not equally distributed throughout the population will be faithfully represented in the total sample.

THE DANGER OF THE BAROMETER APPROACH

At election time political analysts frequently yield to the temptation of dramatizing survey results by limiting the number of geographic areas and singling out counties or precincts or so-called barometer areas. These areas are picked out individually or in combination because they have closely mirrored the national or regional results in previous elections, and it is assumed that the results of the forthcoming election will be indicated by an understanding of these barometer areas. The pitfall of this fascinating approach is that in most cases the accuracy of these barometers for predictive purposes is of limited duration, and there is no way of foretelling just when the barometer areas being used will go awry.

Let the reader suppose he was searching for a barometer for the Presidential election in 1940. Suppose he happened to select each of the five counties listed below because they were fairly close to the national election in the two prior elections. Alas, all five pointed to a Willkie majority (Table 4–3).

What happened in these counties in 1940? We suggest that

since domestic issues were the major considerations in 1932 and 1936 and international issues entered the picture in 1940 in a big way, certain barometer counties, selected because of their similarity of the distribution of their vote in the thirties to the national percentages, went awry in 1940 with the entry of a new major campaign issue. This is not to say that all such barometer counties proved unfaithful in 1940, but the agonizing question haunts: Will the one (or the combination) selected remain faithful this next time?

TABLE 4-3

Counties Selected As Barometers for 1940 Where
Willkie Would Have Been Shown the National Winner
(Republican percentage of the two-party vote)

	1932	1936	1940
National	40.8%	37.5%	45.0%
Cottonwood Co. (Minn.)	40.0	39.0	58.6
Erie Co. (Ohio)	41.6	39.8	54.9
Jackson Co. (Oregon)	42.1	39.3	55.7
Clelan Co. (Washington)	43.3	38.3	52.8
Waukesha Co. (Wisconsin)	38.8	37.3	56.5

A barometer county seeker might have come up with one (or the combination) of the following four counties in 1960 and announced that Richard Nixon would defeat John Kennedy. (See Table 4–4.)

The fact that Nixon's percentages in these counties remained as high as the percentages for the extremely popular Eisenhower and did not drop off to the extent they did nationwide suggests that Kennedy's Roman Catholicism may have been a disadvantage in these "barometer" counties. Another four counties selected would have indicated a Kennedy landslide of 1964 proportions instead of the close result it was nationally. (See Table 4–5.)

TABLE 4-4

*Counties Selected As Barometers for 1960 Where
Nixon Would Have Been Shown the National Winner
(Republican percentage of the two-party vote)*

	1948	1952	1956	1960
National	47.6%	55.4%	57.8%	49.9%
Clay Co. (Indiana)	48.7	53.9	56.1	58.2
St. Francois Co. (Mo.)	46.1	54.6	56.8	58.4
Guilford Co. (N.C.)	45.1	53.4	59.9	57.6
Carroll Co. (Tenn.)	48.5	56.8	56.7	60.4

In these "barometer" counties, Kennedy's religion appears
to have been a strength. The use of one or more of those
counties would have led us to predict a Kennedy landslide of
LBJ-over-Goldwater proportions.

TABLE 4-5

*Counties Selected As Barometers for 1960 Where Kennedy
Would Have Been Shown the Landslide Winner Nationally
(Democratic percentage of the two-party vote)*

	1948	1952	1956	1960
National	52.4%	44.6%	42.2%	50.1%
Windham Co. (Conn.)	53.0	46.4	40.4	57.0
St. Marys Co. (Maryland)	50.5	45.7	44.3	65.1
Worcester Co. (Mass.)	55.6	46.9	39.8	60.6
San Miguel (N.M.)	51.6	45.4	44.1	58.1

The more "barometer" units that can be combined, the more
accurate the emerging picture is likely to be. With large numbers
of barometer areas, the unpredictable factor that will influence
some of them to move off more strongly in one direction will
tend to be offset by those barometer areas that are influenced
strongly in the other direction, and all these bad barometers

will be submerged among the (hopefully) larger number of barometers which remain true. (The average Nixon percentage, when all eight of the above 1960 barometers are combined, is 49.2 compared with the 49.9 percent for Nixon nationally.)

Nevertheless, no matter how many barometer areas are used, there is always the probability that an inordinate number of barometer areas selected will not involve sufficient dynamic elements that go into influencing national elections. Barometer areas may have been indicative in the past because they were the bland undynamic areas from which the larger impact of those more extreme influences that have gone into the balance were absent. The danger lies in these influences coming together in an untraditional way next time—to upset the barometer analysis.

☞ **How a Sample Is Drawn** ☜

For illustrative purposes, let us take the state of Nebraska and set as our task drawing a probability sample of all adults 18 years of age and over. Suppose we want a sample of 500 respondents based upon 50 sampling points.

We start with the very latest data from the United States Census Bureau, which in this case is 1970. The Census lists the population of all counties in Nebraska, as well as the population of all localities within each county. For cities the population is given down to the block level and for other areas the population is given down to the township or precinct level.

The first step is to classify the population of each county by city size. That is, we divide the population of each county into six categories—"strata"—as follows:

I 250,000 and over
II 50,000 to 249,999

III Adjoining urbanized areas
IV 2,500 to 49,999 (excluding places already
      listed in Stratum III)
V Towns and villages under 2,500
VI Open rural country under 2,500

(For large states in which there is one or more large metropolis, an additional stratum is included for cities of one million or over.)

Let us, for example, take Douglas County. (See Table 4–6.) The first stratum includes one city of over 250,000 residents —Omaha, with a population of 347,328. Douglas County contains no cities falling within the 50,000 to 250,000 range, i.e., Stratum II. In Stratum III there are 10 localities in the county.

TABLE 4-6

Population by Strata for Douglas County

I –	347,328
II –	–
III –	25,832
IV –	–
V –	3,917
VI –	12,378

Together their population amounts to 25,832. (See Table 4–7.) No towns qualify for inclusion in Stratum IV. Stratum V and Stratum VI are made up of areas whose combined populations total 3,917 and 12,378, respectively.

This procedure is followed for all 93 counties in Nebraska and the results are put on a master table. (See Table 4–8.)

The counties on Table 4–8 are listed as they fall along a serpentine line that was drawn beginning in the northeast corner of the state—Dakota County—and running through every county in the state. (See Figure 4–1.) This zig-zag line reduces

TABLE 4-7

Population of Localities in Stratum III for Douglas County

		POPULATION
Beechwood Precinct		125
Benson Precinct		1,841
Douglas Precinct		180
Ralston City		4,265
Florence Precinct (the urban part)		45
McCardle Precinct (the urban part)		5,377
Boys Town Village		989
Millard Precinct (the urban part)		2,809
Millard City		7,458
Union Precinct (the urban part)		2,743
	Total	25,832

any sectional bias occurring by chance, as it conceivably might if the counties were listed alphabetically or another way.

Since we plan on 50 sampling points, we divide the total population of the state (1,483,493) by 50 and come up with

TABLE 4-8

County Populations by Strata

COUNTY	STRATA					
	I	II	III	IV	V	VI
Dakota	—	—	7,920	—	2,073	3,144
Thurston	—	—	—	—	3,238	3,704
Burt	—	—	—	—	5,354	3,893
Washington	—	—	—	6,106	2,287	4,917
Douglas	347,328	—	25,832	—	3,917	12,378
Sarpy	—	—	53,771	—	2,352	7,573
Cass	—	—	—	6,371	5,411	6,294
Otoe	—	—	—	7,441	3,290	4,845
Nemaha	—	—	—	3,650	2,383	2,943
Richardson	—	—	—	5,444	2,876	3,966
Pawnee	—	—	—	—	2,218	2,255
Johnson	—	—	—	—	3,109	2,634
Gage	—	—	—	12,389	4,252	9,078
Lancaster	—	149,518	3,925	—	3,687	10,842
Etc.						

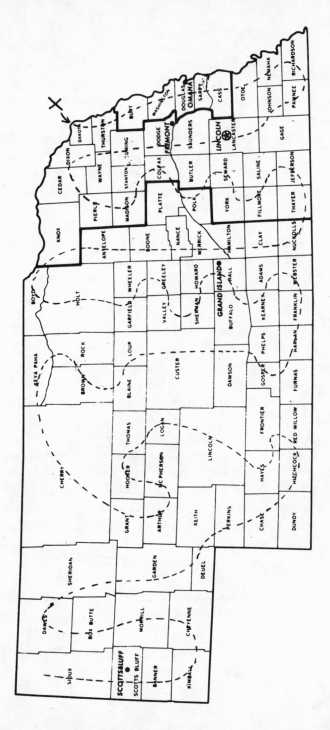

FIGURE 4-1

an interval number (29,670). The first sampling point is determined by a table of random numbers and falls somewhere between zero and the interval number of 29,670. In this case it happened to be 10,480.

We then look at the overall chart (Table 4–8) and commence in Stratum I. We proceed down to Douglas County where we find the number 347,328, which we know represents Omaha. We then turn back to the Census material, which lists the population of each locality in each county. In the case of Omaha, it lists population block by block. We start at the first block listed and look at the block's population. We add to this the number of people residing on the second block, the third block, and so on until the number 10,480 is reached—which was the randomly determined starting point. This block becomes the first sampling point.

To the random starting number we add the interval number —10,480 plus 29,670—and come up with another number, 40,150, which will indicate the second sampling point. Since the population of Omaha has not yet been exhausted, we continue adding block population to block population until the number 40,150 is reached. The block in which this number falls then becomes the second sampling point.

We then add the interval number (29,670) to 40,150 and come up with 69,820, which will be our third sampling point, etc. This procedure is continued until the entire population of Omaha has passed. In this instance, we would have obtained twelve sampling points (out of our intended fifty for Nebraska) in the city of Omaha.

When we are past the total population of Omaha, we go back to the overall chart (Table 4–7) and see there are no more cities in the state falling in Stratum I. So we go on to Stratum II and find that the county of Lancaster contains a city qualifying for Stratum II (which, it will be recalled, is the category for cities between 50,000 and 499,999 in population). In this case, it is the city of Lincoln with a population of 149,518. We proceed through that city's population block by block just as in the case of Omaha and another 5 sampling points fall into our sample.

There being no other cities qualifying for Stratum II in the state, we go on to Stratum III and repeat the process through it and subsequent strata until the 50 sampling points are determined in this way.

We then obtain a map of each sampling point (see Figure 4–2) and interviewers are instructed to start at a specific point —such as the southwest corner of a block. They skip the first household and go on to the next, and so on down the street. The first household is skipped to reduce a bias that might be introduced by overrepresentation of corner houses, which may be untypical of houses within the block. The interviewer will then proceed in a specified direction obtaining one interview in each house until his assignment has been completed.

To insure a purely random selection of individuals living on a specific block, interviewers should really proceed in either of two ways. All inhabitants of voting age on the block could be prelisted and then respondents selected randomly from that listing. Or, the block could be divided into segments containing roughly equal numbers of houses. One segment would then be randomly chosen and persons within households selected in a systematic fashion.

After the potential respondents have been identified, no substitutions are permitted, and interviews must be conducted with each respondent specified. To obtain each interview might require returning to a given household a repeated number of times in order to talk to the specific individual. This process is termed "callbacks." It is a costly process but one which is extremely important in achieving a pure probability sampling of individuals.

The proceeding explanation of the way a sample might be drawn is only one of many sample designs. The Gallup Poll

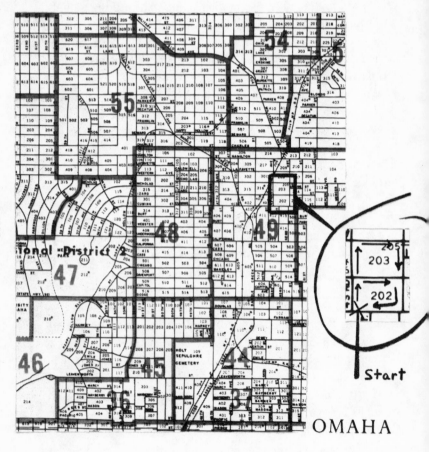

OMAHA

FIGURE 4–2

sample, for instance, is somewhat more complicated than our relatively simple state sample for Nebraska.[8] First, within each of the city-size strata, as described above, the Gallup Poll further stratifies by seven regions: New England, Middle Atlantic, East Central, West Central, South, Mountain, and Pacific States. Secondly, the Gallup Poll sample is based on a pure random selection of interviewing areas.[9] The population data is worked through pretty much as above, with each interval number used as the starting point from which a randomly selected number will indicate the location of the interviewing area.[10] And thirdly, over 300 interviewing areas are thus randomly selected.

☞ Weighting Procedures ☜

A refinement often employed is to introduce various weighting procedures. These procedures are intended to correct known and measurable bias so that the sample is a faithful representation of the population being surveyed. These weighting procedures are not used to introduce bias—as is often alleged. Rather, their intent is to improve the composition of the sample so that it more closely mirrors the characteristics of the population sampled.

For example, people who are less likely to be found at home when the interviewer calls obviously will be undersampled as compared with people who are usually at home most of the time. A statistical method was first suggested over twenty-five years ago by H. O. Hartley in Great Britain and later developed here in this country by Alfred Politz and W. R. Simmons. It is a substitute for the purer but more costly process of returning to the interviewing area a number of times to attempt to interview these hard-to-reach people. It is called the "times at home" technique.[11]

As the technique is sometimes employed, all respondents who are interviewed are asked how many of the three previous days they were at home at the very same time the interview on the fourth day was taking place. Thus, people who were home only once—the day of the interview—are given a weight of four; those at home two out of the four days possible—including the day the interview took place—are given a weight of two; those at home three times are given a weight of one and one-third ($1\frac{1}{3}$); and those at home all four days are given a weight of one.

The sample can also be weighted to place it in line with census data, thereby correcting what would otherwise be a biased sample. For instance, lesser-educated people are likely to be underrepresented in probability-based samples because some of them may feel less confident of their ability to answer questions and a higher refusal rate among them results. Thus, lesser-educated people would be underrepresented in a sample if their group were not weighted to bring the sample in line with census figures on educational distribution.

Sometimes these weighting procedures, or sample corrections, are criticized by laymen as "an unnecessary cooking of the data." Were there to be a mere counting of heads without these weighting refinements, the sample obtained would be biased. To take these steps helps produce an unbiased sample.

Everyone has contact with the national census at least once a decade. Is it not reasonable for people to think they should, therefore, have contact with the national polls equally often? In practice, the Gallup Poll's samples for two years total about 70,000 interviews, or about 350,000 people each decade. The latest census indicates that there are 139,000,000 Americans 18 years of age or over. If this population were to remain static—no one dying, no one aging, no one moving abroad—it would take nearly four centuries—399 years—for interviewers to exhaust the supply of adults to be interviewed for the first time by the Gallup Poll. Thus, it is little wonder so few Americans have been interviewed by any major poll or even know anyone who has.

At a social gathering in Princeton a number of years ago, Dr. Gallup was approached by a lady who asked why she had never been interviewed. He replied that her chances of being interviewed were about as great as her chances of being struck by lightning. Without a moment's hesitation she replied: "But Dr. Gallup, I *have* been struck by lightning!"

Notes

1. See George H. Gallup and E. Hill, *The Secrets of Long Life* (New York: Bernard Geis Associates, 1960).

2. See C. A. Moser, *Survey Methods in Social Investigation* (London: Heinemann, 1958), pp. 100–108.

3. There is often confusion about what "random" means when applied to sampling. Consulting *Webster's Seventh Collegiate Dictionary,* we find the definition most appropriate in this case to be: "Being a member of, consisting of, or relating to a set of elements that have a definite probability of occurring with a specific frequency." This is to be contrasted with the other definition given: "Lacking a definite plan, purpose or pattern." Random sampling is, of course, a plan with a purpose, but not necessarily a perfect pattern. The misleading synonyms for "random" include: *haphazard,* which "applies to what is done without regard for regularity, fitness or ultimate consequence" (random sampling does have a regard for the regularity of its approach and for the ultimate consequence thereof); *casual,* which "suggests working or acting without deliberation, intention or purpose" (random sampling is deliberate and has purpose); and *desultory,* which "implies a jumping or skipping from one thing to another ungoverned by method or system" (random sampling is in itself a method).

4. Sampling error also depends upon the percentage that is obtained in response to a given question. Sampling error is largest when percentages on a question split 50–50 and grows gradually less as the split approaches the 1–99 ratio. To provide the safest estimate of sampling error, it is usually shown at the maximum range, i.e., the 50 percent figure.

POLLS

5. Charles W. Roll, Jr., "Straws in the Wind: The Record of the *Daily News* Poll," *The Public Opinion Quarterly*, 32 (Summer 1968): 251–260.

6. Other considerations might trigger the need for larger numbers of interviews, such as ensuring sufficient coverage of special population segments when survey results must account for them. This need results from the importance of such population segments to the analysis being undertaken, rather than from the size of the overall population under analysis. One polling practitioner, for example, recommends a sample size of 300 for a state such as Vermont and a sample size of 800 for California. He does so on the assumption that the latter state is more complex (e.g., differentiations between northern and southern California are important for political purposes) and, thus, rightly feels more interviews are needed in each portion of the state. We feel he may be selling Vermont a bit short for it, too, has population characteristics that could well justify larger sample sizes if regional or other differences were crucial to the analysis.

7. Like "random," the word "select" as used in the polling profession is a source of some confusion. *Webster's* defines it to mean "to take by preference from a number or group" or "to make a choice." There is no choice or preference in determining which interview area or which persons are to fall into the survey. It is not a matter of judgment. We suggest it is more descriptive of the process to talk about which interviewing areas or individuals "fall into" the sample.

8. See Paul K. Perry, "Election Survey Procedures of the Gallup Poll," *Public Opinion Quarterly* 24 (Fall 1960): 531–542; and Paul K. Perry, "Gallup Poll Election Survey Experience, 1950 to 1960," *Public Opinion Quarterly* 26 (Spring 1962): 272–279.

9. The partial sample of Nebraska as drawn above is technically a systematic sample because the same interval number was used each time for the selection of interviewing areas. A random starting point lends a kind of randomness to the selection, but the purist might insist it not be classified as a random sample, which is one where the selection process is governed by intervals of random size.

10. Actually, two randomly selected localities are drawn from each interval's starting point to produce a replicated sample of localities to enable a more precise pinpointing of the sample's reliability. An advantage of randomly selected interviewing areas over the systematic selection described above for Nebraska is that substitution of interviewing areas is possible when originally selected areas become exhausted by repeated surveys in the same area. In the systematic sample the selection process is locked in to inflexible intervals of equal size. In the random selection process, one randomly selected area can be very easily substituted for a previously selected area that was randomly selected.

11. See H. O. Hartley in discussion of F. Yates, "A Review of Recent Statistical Developments in Sampling Surveys," *Journal of the Royal Statistical Society* A 109 (1946): 12–43; also Alfred Politz and W. R. Simmons, "An Attempt to Get the 'Not at Homes' into the Sample Without Callbacks," *Journal of the American Statistical Association* 44 (March

1949): 9–31; see also Afred Politz and W. R. Simmons, "Note on 'An Attempt to Get the Not At Homes into the Sample Without Callbacks,'" *Journal of the American Statistical Association* 45 (March 1950): 136–37; and W. R. Simmons, "A Plan to Account for 'Not At Homes' by Combining Weighting and Callbacks," *The Journal of Marketing* 19 (1954): 42–53. For a criticism of this technique see Leslie Kish, *Survey Sampling* (New York: John Wiley & Sons, 1967), pp. 559, 560.

5

Poll-Watching: Some Procedural Considerations

THE techniques of opinion polling vary in their complexity from sophisticated statistical computations to the routine and often tedious details of drawing a sample of people to be interviewed. While the basic notion of opinion polling is exceedingly simple, a host of subtleties enter in at each stage of the process. An oversight at any juncture can bias the results of a poll rendering them totally useless—or worse, misleading.

It was Albert Einstein who noted that "the formulation of a problem is often more essential than its solution."[1] This is especially true with the opinion survey, which is a technique applicable in a diversity of situations. Procedures vary with the kind of information that is being sought. Election eve measurements involve procedures markedly different from those employed in assessing the issues at work in a Senate race.

A number of basic decisions are made at the outset in any poll. Early deliberation can save the anguish occasioned by reading a carefully executed survey that does not answer the questions for which it was intended. One such decision is: Who is to be interviewed? The answer may not be as obvious as it may appear in a given situation. Imagine the client interested in assessing the political climate of a state. Does he want to limit interviews only to registered voters, even though this would leave out some additional people who will register and turn out to vote in the election, e.g., the newly enfranchised 18-year-olds in 1972? Or, does he want to interview all adults of voting age, even though time and resources may be squandered in obtaining the views of some people not likely in the end to express themselves at the ballot box?

Another question is: What kind of interview is to be conducted? Increasingly, political polls are done by telephone because they are fast and relatively less expensive than polls based on in-person interviews. Yet, the limitations of telephone interviewing may overshadow these considerations, requiring direct personal interviews to be conducted.

Sample size, too, can be determined only with reference to the specific purposes of the survey. The greater the number of people in the sample, the more reliable the poll—and the greater the cost. There is no point in a client's paying for more precision than he needs, just as there is no point in achieving a false economy that limits unduly the kinds of conclusions that can be drawn from a poll.

What is to be asked of the people interviewed? Since public opinion operates on a number of levels, from deeply held attitudes to momentary views on topical issues, each level must be approached separately. Political polls often tend to focus exclusively upon the "beauty contest" aspects of politics—approval ratings, candidate recognition scores, and the like. Neglected are the more subtle differentiations in the public's perception of issues and candidates. Many polling firms have developed relatively standardized questionnaires that are employed again and again without adequate consideration of the unique needs of each client and the uniqueness of each contest and constituency.

While these decisions about the purpose of a survey seem

obvious enough, they are so often made too hurriedly as a campaign gains momentum, and as a result the information available through the survey is inadequate or not responsive to the need.

In this chapter we will examine four considerations bearing upon the interpretation of surveys that have to do with the procedural aspects of conducting a political poll: what kind of interviews were conducted; what questions were asked; when are results statistically significant; and what the dangers are of drawing inferences that go beyond the data.

☞ Interviewing: By Mail, Telephone, or in Person? ☜

Opinion data can be gathered in three major ways: in person, by telephone, or by mail. Each approach has its advantages and drawbacks.

By all odds, the least expensive way to get information is through the mail questionnaire. In political research, however, mail surveys are not very useful due to the low return of questionnaires mailed out. Even when gimmicks are used, such as the inclusion of cash incentives with the questionnaire and subsequent mailings, the return seldom goes beyond 50 percent in a general population survey. The exception is when special groups are surveyed, such as members of organizations or subscribers to publications. In general, however, it is difficult to ascertain whether people who have returned the questionnaire differ from those who have not, so results may not be representative.[2] This is exactly what is wrong with the mail questionnaires that so many Congressmen make use of.

Telephone or personal interviews are much more satisfactory when it comes to opinion research on public issues or political matters. There are differing judgments within the polling fraternity as to whether telephone interviews are as fruitful as personal interviews.

Telephone interviewing has become quite popular recently in political polling, especially in privately commissioned surveys. Polling for both President Nixon and Senator Muskie, among others, has included wide-scale telephone surveys.

Polls by telephone have three principal attractions: they are cheap, they are quick, and they allow greater dispersion of respondents in the sample. They cost from 50 percent to 60 percent less than a comparable personal interview survey and can be executed within a 24-hour period. As a member of the firm that has conducted telephone surveys for President Nixon commented: "In a day, you can do here what it would take you four weeks to do if you had to mail out questionnaires [to interviewers]."[3]

In our judgment, these attractions are far outweighed by some significant drawbacks. Two of the disadvantages are relatively minor. One is the inability to let respondents peruse exhibits during an interview, such as cards listing problems of concern or displaying rating scales. The other is the difficulty —if not impossibility—of accurately determining a respondent's income level or race over the telephone.

Even more important is the inability of reaching people living in households that have no telephone. Nationally these amount to about 11 percent of all households, but it is appreciably higher in certain areas of the country (e.g., 35 percent in Mississippi) and in certain population groups.[4]

A Gallup Poll in January 1972 indicated that about 90 percent of American households had telephones. Table 5–1 indicates the difference in telephone ownership by various population groups.

Specifically, nonwhite citizens, people in the southern states, those with lower incomes, the lesser-educated, younger adults, and people in small communities or rural areas are less likely to have telephones than their counterparts in the population.

TABLE 5-1

Distribution of Telephone Ownership by Population Group

	WITH TELEPHONES	WITHOUT TELEPHONES
Race		
White	91%	9%
Nonwhite	85	15
Region		
North	94	6
South	81	19
Household Income		
$15,000 and over	98	2
$10,000 to $14,999	96	4
$7,000 to $9,999	92	8
$5,000 to $6,999	88	12
Under $5,000	78	22
Education		
College	95	5
High school	91	9
Grade school	84	16
Age		
18 to 29 years	86	14
30 to 49 years	93	7
50 years and over	91	9
Community Size		
500,000 and over	94	6
2,500 to 499,999	90	10
Under 2,500	85	15

What does this mean in terms of biasing a sample? Based on the distribution of various population segments in the above mentioned Gallup Poll on telephone ownership, it means that when interviews are conducted by telephone at least an additional 5 people out of every 100 interviewed are in the $7,000 or over income category and at least 5 less per 100 interviewed are in the under $7,000 income category than we can expect in the more perfectly balanced personal in-home interview sample. Similar differences would also appear for regional, educational, racial, age, and community size distributions, although in lesser degree.

But, someone rejoins, this is really very small and certainly falls within sampling error range anyway. True it is not a shattering shortcoming, but telephone sampling bias, when compounded with expected sampling error, has caused many preelection measurements to look fairly silly.

In partisan situations, because of the nature of the population groups with higher telephone ownership, the Republican side usually receives a 4 or 5 point advantage it should not receive.

The most disturbing deficiency of telephone surveys is the reluctance of respondents to venture into controversial areas on the phone. Without the rapport established in the personal interview, there is a tendency for some people to give less negative answers, particularly when it comes to their views of political personalities. This was demonstrated in a survey of Republicans in Westchester County, New York, in May 1970. Telephone and personal interviews were conducted at the same time with comparable samples. The same questions were used. It turned out that the Republicans interviewed by telephone were less likely to be critical of the way President Nixon was handling his job as President in general and his handling of Vietnam in particular. (See Table 5–2.)

It could be argued that this patterning of responses was a fluke and those interviewed by telephone just happened to have a higher opinion of the President than those interviewed personally. Table 5–3 shows, however, that the same pattern was repeated in the case of the job rating assigned Congressman Ogden Reid, who was then under fire in conservative circles for not being sufficiently supportive of the President.

In this same survey, there was no difference between the telephone and personal interviews when it came to the preference

TABLE 5-2

Nixon Overall Rating

Those Interviewed:	EXCEL- LENT OR GOOD	ONLY FAIR OR POOR	NO OPINION	
By Telephone	72%	24%	4%	100%
Personally*	56	38	6	100%

Nixon Vietnam Rating

Those Interviewed	APPROVE	DIS- APPROVE	NO OPINION	
By Telephone	69%	25%	6%	100%
Personally*	55	38	7	100%

*In order to make the samples exactly comparable, people without telephones were excluded from the personal interview group.

TABLE 5-3

Reid Overall Rating

Those Interviewed:	EXCEL- LENT OR GOOD	ONLY FAIR OR POOR	NO OPINION	
By Telephone	71%	20%	9%	100%
Personally*	55	30	15	100%

*In order to make the samples exactly comparable, people without telephones were excluded from the personal interview group.

between Congressman Reid and his primary election opponent. But this makes perfect sense: the question involving a choice between two candidates can be answered without a respondent's having to say anything negative about one of them.

Further evidence of a bias toward less negative data in telephone polling comes when comparing the results of an all-personal interview survey of the Gallup Poll with an all-telephone interview survey by Opinion Research Corporation, which does much of the survey work for the national Republican Party.

Surveying in 1,556 homes (beginning July 16 through 19 of 1971), the Gallup Poll found that 49 percent of Americans 18 years of age or over approved "of the way Nixon is handling his job as President," with 38 percent disapproving, and 13 percent unable to say. Telephoning 1,002 Americans 18 or over (between July 20 and 21 of 1971), Opinion Research Corporation found that 54 percent approved "of the way Richard Nixon is handling his job as President" to 32 percent disapproving and 14 percent unable to say.[5] (See Table 5–4.)

TABLE 5-4

Nixon Popularity

NIXON'S HANDLING OF PRES. JOB	GALLUP POLL IN-HOME INTERVIEWS (JULY 16-19, 1971)	ORC TELEPHONE (JULY 20-21, 1971)
Approve	49%	54%
Disapprove	38	32
Can't say	13	14

The margin for approval is 11 points in the Gallup Poll but 22 points in the O.R.C. survey. A part of the difference is attributable to a telephone sample, which we have indicated is likely to under-represent young people, poorer people, and the lesser educated, all of whom are more likely to be oriented

101

toward the Democratic Party. But the major part of the difference probably is attributable to the reluctance of some people to be quite as negative as they would like when dealing with unseen strangers at the other end of the telephone line.

While the differences are not wide, they pinpoint further the problem of telephone interviewing. And this case is a good example of what the reader should be aware of when various polls are tersely compared in the press during a campaign period.

Telephone surveys can be well used to get a quick reading on the public's response to a major speech or event. However, when the purpose is to marshal information around which a campaign strategy can be formed, personal interviews are much preferable.

When personal interviews are used in a survey, the question is often asked: How can you be sure the interviews that are turned in are really valid and have not been fabricated by the interviewer in his own living room? There is little future for the dishonest interviewer; sooner or later he is usually found out. The careful research organization will usually follow-up interviews with some form of validation. Business reply postals are sent to selected respondents after each survey, asking if they were interviewed and whether they were asked a specific question at the beginning of the interview, toward the middle, and at the end. When something suspicious turns up, a further probe is made by telephone to all respondents covered by the interviewer whose work has been called into question.

Further, there are added to most questionnaires so-called "cheater" questions which are designed so that the delinquent or dishonest interviewer betrays himself in the way they are completed. When all signs point to falsification of interviews by an interviewer, all interviews conducted by that person are discarded. However, less than three percent of the interviewers who complete their training ever turn up as "cheaters."

👉 *The Art of Asking Questions*[6] 👈

A poll is only as good as the questions it asks. Since people will generally try to answer any question put to them in a survey, a client's input in the drafting of questions is essential. Yet, it is here that the client is so often left out or not able to play a meaningful role.

There are two basic types of questions. The so-called "open" questions are those that pose some problem or topic and ask respondents what they think about it. An example would be the frequently asked question in the national polls: "What problems that the government in Washington has to deal with are you, yourself, most concerned or worried about?" The free flowing response is then recorded by an interviewer verbatim.

This type of question is to be contrasted to the "closed" question in which specific response alternatives are provided and the person interviewed is asked to choose that alternative closest to his own view. A closed form of the previous example would be: "Here is a card on which are listed a number of problems that the government in Washington has to deal with. Please look the card over carefully and tell me which two or three of the problems listed you, yourself, are most concerned or worried about?" The card handed to the respondent would list problems such as: unemployment, rising prices and the high cost of living, Vietnam, water and air pollution, civil rights and racial tensions, etc. So that the priority of problems listed will not bias the results, ideally the order is changed randomly for different segments of the sample of people interviewed.

Open questions are useful when the dimensions of the public's view are not readily apparent. If one were trying to find out what the public's image of a candidate were, one would want to learn what words and phrases people spontaneously suggest to describe him. Presenting respondents with a predetermined set of adjectives would not be so useful since the adjectives may not be those the public regards as applicable, but may be just those that occur to an enthusiastic campaign staff or distant pollster.

When it comes to many other information needs, however, the open questions have less utility. They tend to elicit a dribble of responses that must later be crystallized into some intelligible pattern—a process which may introduce the particular bias of whoever is doing the survey. For example, little was probably gained from this series of vague open questions we came across being used in one of the midwestern states:

"Is there anything in particular that you like about the Democratic Party? What is that?"

"Is there anything in particular that you dislike about the Democratic Party? What is that?"

"Is there anything in particular that you like about the Republican Party? What is that?"

"Is there anything in particular that you dislike about the Republican Party? What is that?"

Open questions are more expensive than closed questions since additional staff time is required for the laborious job of coding these free responses so as to fit them into major categories of response. The additional cost is sometimes well worth it if an open question can be used to shed light on responses to closed questions by asking people why they feel as they do. The need is for balance, however, and this is achieved only in reference to the purposes of the survey.

The problem of framing response alternatives in closed questions is to reduce as far as possible the introduction of bias. This means all the positions or alternatives stated should be along only one dimension of an issue.[7] If respondents were presented with only the following two options for the United States in

Vietnam, they would be legitimately miffed: "The U.S. should withdraw all its forces because the South Vietnamese can now defend themselves *or* the U.S. should keep some forces in Vietnam until the South Vietnamese are able to defend themselves." Nowhere is there a place for the respondent who favors the withdrawal of all U.S. forces and does not care whether the South Vietnamese can defend themselves or not.

Another factor is reducing bias in question wording to ensure that the consequences of one or another of the alternatives are made explicit. Take, for example, a Gallup Poll question: "A proposal has been made in Congress to require the U.S. Government to bring home all U.S. troops before the end of this year (1971). Would you like to have your Congressman vote for or against this proposal?" The choice was an easy one as evidenced by the 66 percent favoring the proposal, the 26 percent opposing it, with only the remaining 8 percent having no opinion. This was only part of the story, however. A follow-up question was asked of those favoring the proposal: "Some people say that the U.S. should withdraw all its troops from Vietnam by the end of this year (1971), regardless of what happens there after U.S. troops leave. Do you agree or disagree?" The 66 percent favoring withdrawal on the first question divided 41 percent still urging withdrawal, 18 percent dropping off and opposing withdrawal, and 7 percent having no opinion. Thus, the more faithful portrayal of opinion was not the initial 66–26 split favorable to withdrawal. It was that 41 percent of the public favored withdrawal regardless of what happened in Vietnam, and 44 percent opposed withdrawal without assurances that South Vietnam could stand on its own, with 15 percent undecided.

Exemplary of a question which poses the consequences of alternative courses of action in Vietnam is the following. "Suppose the United States were confronted with a choice of only the two alternatives listed on this card, which one would you rather have the United States follow? (1) End the war by accepting the best possible compromise settlement even though it might sooner or later allow the Vietnamese Communists to take over control of South Vietnam. (2) Fight on until a settlement can be reached which will insure that the Communists do not get control of South Vietnam."[8]

In the wording of questions, it is desirable to use easy conversational language so that the interview will flow smoothly. Since 45 percent of Americans 25 years of age and over have not completed high school, readily understandable words must be employed.[9] Thus, if a question was intended to assess the degree of public concern over what observers characterize as "a crisis of confidence in our institutions," the wording would have to be something like "our traditional way of doing things is not working and some basic changes are needed if we are to work together."[10]

A recurring dilemma in survey research is how to measure opinion on an issue about which public understanding may be limited. There is often a need to explain an issue or problem with several sentences added as a preamble to the question itself. We shall address this point at length later in Chapter Six.

A special aspect of the vocabulary problem is to ensure that the language used in a question means the same things to all people interviewed. An amusing example comes from an early Gallup Poll in which people were asked if they owned any "stock." A surprisingly high degree of "stock" ownership turned up in interviews in the southwest where respondents were naturally thinking of livestock. The question had to be reworded to make reference to "securities or stock listed on any stock exchange."

Difficulties in question wording are also presented when the names of prestige political figures or revered institutions are introduced. An experiment was done in the early days of polling which illustrates this. Comparable samples of respondents were simultaneously asked two questions about Presidential succession. One sample was asked: "Would you favor or oppose *adding a law* to the Constitution preventing a President from succeeding himself more than once?" The other sample was asked: "Would you favor or oppose *changing* the Constitution in order to prevent a President from succeeding himself more than once?" To the first question, 50 percent of the respondents answered in the negative; to the second question, 65 percent in the negative. Thus, the public would rather "add to" than "change" the Constitution.[11]

Bias can also enter in through the sequence in which questions appear on a questionnaire. To check against this, three rules generally apply. First, the open questions should precede closed questions on the same subject. Thus, one would want to ask the open question about what people felt were the most important questions facing the country before getting to closed questions about specific issues related to those national problems.

For much the same reason, a more general question on a given subject should precede a more specific question, even if both are closed questions. Thus, people should be asked about President Nixon's overall handling of "his job as President" before being asked specifically about his handling of Vietnam.

The third general consideration is that when two questions are likely to bias each other equally, the more important question is put first. This is not an uncommon occurrence. For example, a respondent would be asked first who he would like to see win the Presidential election, second whether he approves or disapproves of the job President Nixon is doing, and only third whether he considers himself a Democrat, a Republican or Independent.

To illustrate, an October 1971 Gallup Poll reported President Nixon obtaining 43 percent of the vote against Senator Muskie and Governor Wallace, with his approval rating standing at 54 percent and with 25 percent of the public identifying themselves as Republicans. To have placed the party identification question first would have biased the subsequent two questions. This is because the advantage the Democratic party has over the Republican party in terms of the number of people who so identify themselves is usually much greater than any advantage, if any, the Democratic candidate has over the Republican candidate. Since people identifying themselves as Democrats would have revealed their party loyalty to the interviewer, they might feel constrained to opt for the Democratic candidate. Similarly, putting the job rating question first would result in some respondents saying they approved of the job the President was doing, feeling constrained to select him in a trial heat question.

Clues that bias is being introduced are usually uncovered quickly when a questionnaire is tried out on a limited number of trial respondents, or "pretested." Trained interviewers can determine the extent to which questions work and their sequence influences patterns of response. Even then, however, one cannot always be totally confident that a certain amount of bias has not been unknowingly imparted. With care and experience, however, bias can at least be minimized. It is because of the present danger of bias that reports of survey results should always include the *exact* wording of questions so that the reader can judge the fairness and adequacy of the questions for himself.

☞ When Are Differences Significant? ☜

Among poll findings that are the most fascinating to watch are trends in opinion. The trends most closely watched are those regarding Presidential popularity and the relative standing of candidates. Trends can also be exceedingly informative on substantive issues, documenting turns in the public's view of issues.

Table 5–5 shows such a trend with respect to the Gallup Poll question of whether or not "the United States made a mistake sending troops to fight in Vietnam."

TABLE 5-5

Percent Feeling U.S. Had Made a Mistake
Sending Troops to Vietnam

1965	August	24%
1966	March	25
	May	36
	September	35
	November	31
1967	February	32
	May	37
	July	41
	October	46
	December	45
1968	February	46
	March	49
	April	48
	August	53
	October	54
1969	March	52
	September	58
1970	January	57
	April	51
	June	56
1971	January	59
	May	61

Obviously, for such trends to make any sense, they must be based upon the same question being asked of completely comparable samples. Under these circumstances, then, what constitutes a meaningful shift in opinion from one sounding to another?

The reader will recall that a margin must be determined for a reported percent to allow for probable sampling error. Similarly, when the results of two separate surveys are being compared, a margin must be allowed that takes into account the probable sampling error of *both* samples.

For the reader's reference, we have included in Table 5–6 the margins that must be allowed when comparing results of two surveys. The table is used in the following manner. The size of the two samples is first determined. One reads down in the column nearest the size of the first sample and across in the row nearest the size of the second sample. The number thus found is the margin that must be allowed *between* the two percentages reported in the two surveys. When the reported percentages tend toward 50 percent, the lower half of the table is used; when they tend toward 20 percent or 80 percent, the upper half of the table is used. This is because there is a chance of larger sampling error when opinion divides about evenly—that is, near the 50 percent mark.[12]

Table 5–6 can also be used to determine what margins must be allowed for differences *within a single survey,* say between Democrats and Republicans or between young and old. In this instance, one first determines the proportion that each of the subgroups under consideration represents, i.e., how many respondents in the overall sample were Democrats and how many were Republicans, to follow through with the example. This proportion, therefore, tells the sample size for each of the subgroups. One then proceeds as before, locating the column closest to the size of the sample of Democrats and the row closest to the size of the sample of Republicans.[13]

While these procedures seem elaborate, they represent the only sound basis for drawing important conclusions regarding differences between surveys or within a single survey. While the nationally syndicated polls of Gallup and Harris are usually based upon samples of 1,500 respondents, most privately commissioned polls have samples of much smaller size. Thus, the margins that need to be allowed in these smaller sample surveys are considerably larger than in the published national polls. Also, when it comes to analysis of differences within one survey, the privately commissioned polls seldom have a sufficient number of respondents in the sample for exceedingly fine differentiations between sample subgroups. When differences between segments of the population assume major importance to a political client, a larger sample may become worth the added cost.

TABLE 5-6

Recommended Allowances for Probable Sampling Error of a Difference between Two Percentages *
(in percentage points)

For Percentages Near 20% or 80%

SIZE OF SAMPLE II	SIZE OF SAMPLE I				
	1,500	750	600	400	200
1,500	4				
750	4	5			
600	5	5	6		
400	6	6	6	7	
200	8	8	8	8	10

For Percentages Near 50%

SIZE OF SAMPLE II	SIZE OF SAMPLE I				
	1,500	750	600	400	200
1,500	5				
750	5	6			
600	6	7	7		
400	7	7	8	8	
200	10	10	10	10	12

*At the 95 percent level of confidence; based on sampling error calculated from experience with the Gallup sample.

☞ Going Beyond the Data ☜

"You must let the data speak to you." This remark from a well-known practitioner reflects the temptation to read more into poll findings than cold percentages portray. While political judgment is essential for good political research, it is better to introduce it at the beginning of a poll when questions are being designed rather than to draw sweeping conclusions about what the data "really mean" after the study is completed.

Politicians are particularly prone to go beyond the data when they see in poll results hints as to the direction a campaign can take. If polls indicate the public is particularly concerned about a given issue, it may be self-defeating for a candidate to pursue the issue without a greater feel for how the public views it. This was seen in the 1970 Congressional elections. The Nixon Administration had obviously been impressed by survey findings that indicated the public's anxiety over unrest on the campuses and elsewhere. It erred significantly—as the election returns evidenced—in the strident oratory that characterized its treatment of these issues. The public was indeed concerned about lawlessness and disorder, but it wanted something positive and constructive.

This conclusion is borne out in an earlier study the authors did in early 1971. In a survey of the American public, we found a marked increase in concern about the problem of "national disunity and political instability." Anxiety about the problem had more than trebled since a similar study was conducted in 1964.[14] When we probed to find out what people regarded as lying behind this unrest, we found that the public was quite alert to some of the larger causes of our national difficulties and not willing to dismiss them just merely as the work of radicals and demonstrators.[15]

Specifically, we presented respondents with a card on which

were listed six causes for the unrest: three were couched in terms of basic systemic problems the country faces, three in terms of protesters and demonstrators. As Table 5–7 shows, the public selected five of the six reasons about equally. However, we ran a special tabulation. We divided respondents into three categories: those who selected reasons relating only to systemic causes; those who selected reasons relating only to protesters, and those who selected a mix of the two. We found that the public divided into the three categories about evenly: 33 percent protesters and demonstrators; 30 percent looking to larger causes; and 30 percent a mix, with the remaining 7 percent having no opinion.

The moral here is that, while there was much appeal to

TABLE 5-7

Reasons for National Unrest Selected

System Related Reasons	
Our traditional way of doing things is not working and some basic changes are needed if we are to work together	34%
Our leaders in government and business are not trying hard enough to solve the problems we face and people are losing confidence in them	31
Many of the problems our country faces are so big that we can't agree on how to solve them	19
Protester Related Reasons	
Some young people have gotten out of hand and have no respect for authority	32
The protests are largely communist inspired	31
Some Negroes and other minorities are making unreasonable demands	31
No Opinion	7

NOTE:
The order of these items on the card was randomized to reduce bias. Also respondents were asked which one or two reasons of the six they felt to be "mainly responsible for this unrest and ill-feeling." Thus, there were many multiple responses.

blaming youth, minorities, and Communists for our woes, the public was looking for something on the positive side. Proposals to ameliorate the causes of the problem were lacking from the Republican campaign and therein lay the disappointing showing on election day in the 1970 congressional races.

Even on the local level, serious miscalculations can follow from going beyond the data. In a 1965 poll for the Democratic organization of Somerset County in New Jersey, a question was asked about the county's educational facilities. People were asked whether they would prefer the county government to wait until Federal and State money was available to build both a vocational school and a junior college or whether they would rather the county go ahead now with the vocational school and defer the junior college until a later date. The results showed the majority (57 percent) of the public wanted to go ahead on their own with the vocational school while less than a quarter (22 percent) wanted to wait until both could be built with Federal and State money.

Upon the basis of this finding, the Democratic organization prevailed upon a popular county official to unveil as her key campaign proposal, a week before the election, models of a huge complex that included not only the desired vocational school, but also a new jail and other county buildings. In a poll two months before the election, she had twice the strength of her Republican challenger. However, cost-conscious voters were so dismayed at the scale of the undertaking she had proposed that she was defeated on election day. (See Table 5–8.)

The considerations spelled out in this chapter have dealt with aspects of the survey technique that have a bearing upon the kinds of inferences that can be drawn from survey data. Another set of considerations also applies having to do with what experience teaches—what one seasoned in the analysis of survey data learns about the dynamics of public opinion. These considerations derive less from set rules laid down by statistical

TABLE 5-8

Freeholder Candidate Choice in
Somerset County, New Jersey, 1965

	SEPTEMBER POLL	ELECTION RESULTS
Grace Gurisic, Democrat	50%	46%
John Ewing, Republican	25	54
Other & undecided	25	—

theory or methodological decisions than they do from experience in working with poll findings. It is to these we turn in the next chapter.

Notes

1. A. Einstein and L. Infeld, *The Evolution of Physics,* (New York: Simon & Schuster, 1942), p. 95.

2. For a detailed presentation of this method, see Paul L. Erdos, *Professional Mail Surveys* (New York: McGraw-Hill, 1970).

3. Robert K. McMillan of Chilton Research Services as quoted in Andrew J. Glass, "Candidates Use Opinion Polls to Plan Campaigns for 1972," *National Journal* 3, No. 33 (August 14, 1971): 170–174.

4. Source: *Pocket Data Book 1971,* Bureau of the Census, Government Printing Office, 1971, p. 294.

5. The Gallup Poll figures and the O.R.C. figures were set forth in "Report on the Polls," Republican National Committee Research Division, July 27, 1971, p. 284.

6. We have borrowed this title from Stanley L. Payne, *The Art of Asking Questions* (Princeton: Princeton University Press, 1951), a classic treatment of the difficulties of question-wording.

7. In presenting response alternatives that state amount or degree, one trick learned through experience is to offer an even number of choices so as to reduce the ease with which a respondent can select the

middle choice. For example, "How much trust and confidence do you have in President Nixon in the way he is handling the FBI—a great deal, a fair amount, not very much, or none at all?"

8. The wording of this question was by Lloyd A. Free and appears in Albert H. Cantril and Charles W. Roll, Jr., *Hopes and Fears of the American People* (New York: Universe Books, 1971), pp. 37–38.

9. This figure seems high, but it is based on data from the U.S. Census Bureau from 1969. While 34 percent of the American people 25 years of age and over have completed high school, 17.1 percent have attended but not completed high school. Add to these people who have attended (but not completed) high school, the 27.8 percent who have not attended high school at all, and the total is 44.9 percent. Source: *Pocket Data Book 1971,* Bureau of the Census, Government Printing Office, 1971, p. 161.

10. Cantril and Roll, *Hopes and Fears,* pp. 32–33.

11. Hadley Cantril, *Gauging Public Opinion* (Princeton: Princeton University Press, 1944), p. 44. (Reprinted by Kennikat Press, 1972.)

12. For example, let us say 50 percent of the respondents in one survey selected a given response alternative and 40 percent of the respondents in a second survey selected the same alternative in reply to the exact same questions. This would amount to a difference of 10 percentage points between the two surveys. Since both percentages are near 50, and assuming both surveys were based upon samples of 1,500, one would consult the lower portion of Table 5–6. Reading down in the column headed "1,500" to the row designated "1,500" one would find the number "5," which is the allowance that must be made to conclude that the difference between the two surveys is statistically significant. Thus, in our example, the shift of ten percentage points is a significant one. Suppose, however, that two surveys reported figures of 22 percent and 24 percent respectively on the same response alternative. We would then consult the upper half of Table 5–6 (for percentages near 20 or 80). Again, assuming samples of 1,500 respondents for both surveys and consulting the upper table, the margin that would have to be allowed is four percentage points. We could thus not conclude that the difference between the 22 percent and the 24 percent was statistically significant. These tables were computed by Paul K. Perry, President of The Gallup Organization, and we are indebted to him for permission to include them.

13. Suppose that, nationally, Democrats comprise about 41 percent of the sample and Republicans about 27 percent. This means, with 1,500 people in the overall sample, there will be about 600 Democrats and 400 Republicans. Since sample composition is necessary to make these computations, privately commissioned polls should always have this information appended to them.

14. These earlier studies were done by the Institute for International Social Research in 1959 and 1964 and reported in Hadley Cantril, *The Pattern of Human Concerns* (New Brunswick: Rutgers University Press, 1965), and Lloyd A. Free and Hadley Cantril, *The Political Beliefs of Americans* (New Brunswick: Rutgers University Press, 1967).

15. Cantril and Roll, *Hopes and Fears,* pp. 32–36.

6

Poll-Watching: Some Interpretive Considerations

> My good judgment comes from experience, and experience—well, that comes from poor judgment.
>
> A KENTUCKY FARMER

THERE is nothing immutable about the results of a poll. The way polls are treated by the press and politicians, one might be led to think otherwise. However, what a poll provides is a picture of the public's view at only one point in time and on only the questions that were asked. Yet, inferences of sweeping proportion are frequently drawn from a poll, leading to fundamental misunderstandings of what the state of public opinion really is.

There are a number of reasons why this is so. Experience teaches that some opinions are more abiding than others and less susceptible to being influenced by events. Similarly, seeming inconsistencies in the mood of the public often yield new insight into the dynamics of the underlying opinion base as they are explained. In this chapter we explore some of the factors experience teaches are important in weighing survey data.

117

☞ The Fluidity and Stability of Opinion ☜

Probably the most traumatic event the U.S. public has had to deal with on the international scene in recent years was the Tet Offensive in Vietnam in early 1968. It proved to be the catalytic event leading those advocating escalation to question the efficacy of military measures and demonstrating to others that the U.S. had a lot farther to go in Indochina than the public had been led to believe.

Yet, in spite of what turned out to be a deep shock to the public, the Tet Offensive was met with an initial public response of marked "hawkishness." It was only with time that this upsurge of militant sentiment dissipated and that the public looked for a way to end the hostilities quickly. This opinion movement has been effectively recorded by the Gallup Poll. The question was asked: "People are called 'hawks' if they want to step up our military effort in Vietnam. They are called 'doves' if they want to reduce our military effort in Vietnam. How would you describe yourself—as a 'hawk' or a 'dove'?" The trend was dramatic. (See Table 6–1.) Immediately after the offensive the percentage calling themselves "hawks" jumped nine percentage points, only to drop twenty points by March and thirty points by November.

In the effort to "be on top of things," there is often a rush to obtain opinion data about events such as the offensive. Table 6–1 shows the dangers of rushing ahead with a survey before opinion has begun to jell in a stabilized way. A public official would have been seriously misled had he allowed the February poll results to guide him in any way. Even two centuries ago, George Washington recognized "it is on *great* occasions *only* and after time has been given for cool and deliberate reflection that the *real* voice of the people can be known."[1] So poll find-

118

ings just after major events will not usually have the lasting significance often attributed to them.

There is also a danger in reading too much into poll data too far in advance of elections. In November 1971, a year before the election, *The New York Times* highlighted the fact that Tom McCall, Governor of Oregon, was the favorite among Republicans over incumbent Senator Mark Hatfield. They cited a poll showing Hatfield drawing only 34.8 percent against McCall's showing of 55.8 percent. The *Times* also reported Congresswoman Edith Green and former Congressman Duncan running ahead of former Senator Wayne Morse by about eleven points on the Democratic side. When Oregonians were asked their overall preference in the Senate race, McCall defeated any Democrat, and Congresswoman Green defeated Senator Hatfield.

TABLE 6-1

Trend on Hawk-Dove Identification

DATES OF INTERVIEWING	PEOPLE DESCRIBING THEMSELVES AS:			
	HAWK	DOVE	NO OPINION	
December 9-13, 1967	52%	35%	13%	100%
Tet Offensive				
February 3-7, 1968	61	23	16	100
March 16-20, 1968	41	42	17	100
October, 1968	44	42	14	100
End of All Bombing of North				
Mid-November, 1968	31	55	14	100

Aside from current interest, there is little basis in these findings to warrant any important decisions being made. The two-way underdog in these findings, Senator Hatfield, mindful of earlier preelection situations in Oregon, wisely reacted: "I've seen polls that indicated one thing and the results came out differently in the election."[2]

Volatility in candidate preferences occurs most frequently in primary election situations where traditional party loyalty is not a factor working to limit the extent of opinion change as it does in general elections. Again, taking the state of Oregon, the 1964 Republican Presidential situation showed much movement prior to the primary. (See Table 6–2.)

TABLE 6-2

Republican Candidate Choice in Oregon, 1964

	FEBRUARY	APRIL	MAY (PRIMARY)
Richard Nixon	23%	15%	17%
Barry Goldwater	20	17	17
Nelson Rockefeller	17	18	33
Henry Cabot Lodge	13	37	28
All others	12	8	5
Undecided	15	5	—

In March, Henry Cabot Lodge, then Ambassador in Saigon, had won a stunning victory among New Hampshire Republicans and, thus, the upward swing in Oregon between the February and April polls. However, when he continued to refuse to express any interest in the nomination, his standing dropped by primary election day. Nelson Rockefeller was the only contestant to campaign actively in the state and to make personal appearances, justifying the use of the appealing slogan: "He cared enough to come" (to Oregon). Rockefeller, who had started with only 17 percent support, went on to win the primary.

As fluid as this situation appears in overall terms, internal switches offsetting each other indicate an even higher degree of volatility. (See Table 6–3.) For these reasons, primary election polling should be viewed with considerably more caution than polls involving general elections.

Even in general election campaigns, however, until the very end polls are much like snapshots taken in the backstretch of a horse race. Such a photograph tells you nothing about what will happen at the finish line. A sequence of photos might allow you to project a winner, but even then the apparent victor may stumble just short of the finish line. These early poll findings of a trial heat nature are fun to watch, but they are certainly no basis upon which to make political commitments or firm decisions regarding campaign strategy.

TABLE 6-3

Internal Switches in Oregon Republican Candidate Choice, 1964

	STANDING IN FEBRUARY POLL	SUPPORT GAINED	SUPPORT LOST	STANDING IN APRIL POLL
Nixon	23%	2% from Goldwater 1% from Lodge, Rockefeller & others 1% from undecided Total Gain of 4%	7% to Lodge 3% to Rockefeller 1% to Goldwater 1% to others & undecided Total Loss of 12%	15%
Goldwater	20	1% from Nixon 1% from Rockefeller 1% from Lodge & others 3% from undecided Total Gain of 6%	4% to Lodge 2% to Nixon 1% to Rockefeller 1% to others 1% to undecided Total Loss of 9%	17
Rockefeller	17	3% from Nixon 1% from Lodge 1% from Goldwater 2% from others 2% from undecided Total Gain of 9%	6% to Lodge 1% to Goldwater 1% to Nixon, others & undecided Total Loss of 8%	18
Lodge	13	7% from Nixon 6% from Rockefeller 4% from Goldwater 5% from others 5% from undecided Total Gain of 27%	1% to Rockefeller 1% to Nixon, Goldwater & others 1% to undecided Total Loss of 3%	37

Public opinion is not, however, always so fluid. Generally, the more basic the level of concerns polls are focusing on, the more stable the findings that are turned up. In our 1971 study, we found a basic stability among the American people when it came to their fundamental hopes and fears. When set against the previous soundings in 1959 and 1964, using the exact same questions, the patterning of hopes and fears have changed little. The overarching concerns continue to be good health, a better standard of living, peace, the achievement of aspirations for one's children, a good job, and a happy family life.[3]

When some topic or issue becomes clearly relevant to concerns that are basic to the public, it can spark a shift in opinion about that topic. That is the reason candidates should focus more on opinion surveys at the basic level of concerns and less on the beauty contest aspects that attract so much attention.

☞ Levels of Opinion ☜

The point that public opinion operates on a number of different levels simultaneously deserves amplification.

Not only is there a range of levels of opinion from basic hopes and fears to topical matters and candidate preferences, but other factors are at work. An example of this was the 1964 Presidential campaign. This race was unique in its pitting of Lyndon Johnson—architect of the Great Society—against Barry Goldwater—the first modern day conservative to be tested in a Presidential contest. The issue that divided them was the classic issue, held over from New Deal days, of how far the Federal Government should go in solving our national social problems. It was the issue that has divided the orthodox Democrat from the orthodox Republican for years.

Lloyd Free and Hadley Cantril came up with an important finding in their study of the political psychology of Americans during this period when they found that when the public's view on the issue was assessed in essentially *ideological* terms, the public tended to be quite conservative and bearish about too large an involvement for the Federal Government. Whereas when people were asked about *specific Federal programs,* they tended to support them in overwhelming proportions.

Specifically, people were asked whether they agreed or disagreed with a number of propositions which were couched in distinctly ideological terms: "the Federal Government is interfering too much in state and local matters," "we should rely more on individual initiative and ability and not so much on government welfare programs," etc. People were then asked whether they approved of specific Federal programs: "a broad general program of Federal aid to education," "a compulsory medical insurance program covering hospital and nursing care for the elderly," etc.

Depending upon the pattern of an individual's replies, he was classified along a spectrum from "liberal" to "conservative" on each of the two batteries of questions. The results were fascinating, showing that fully one-half of the public qualified as "conservatives" on the level of ideology, while nearly two-thirds qualified as "liberals" when it came to support for specific programs of the Federal Government.[4] (See Table 6-4.)

TABLE 6-4

Liberalism-Conservatism on
Ideological and Programmatic Levels

	IDEOLOGICAL		SPECIFIC PROGRAMS	
Completely liberal	4%	} 16%	44%	} 65%
Predominantly liberal	12		21	
Middle-of-the-road		34		21
Predominantly conservative	20	} 50	7	} 14
Completely conservative	30		7	

When the two batteries of questions were cross-tabulated against one another, nearly half (46 percent) of those qualifying as "conservatives" on the ideological level also qualified as "liberals" with respect to their support for specific Federal programs. (See Table 6–5.)

TABLE 6-5

Ideological vs. Programmatic Positions

	IDEOLOGICAL POSITION		
	LIBERAL	MIDDLE-OF-THE-ROAD	CONSER-VATIVE
Support for Specific Federal Programs			
Liberal	90%	78%	46%
Middle-of-the-road	9	18	28
Conservative	1	4	26
	100	100	100

This study of the 1964 election concluded: "While the old argument about the 'welfare state' has long since been resolved at the operational level of government programs, it most definitely *has not* been resolved at the ideological level."[5]

Thus, the reader is cautioned to look closely at the types of nerve endings being touched by a question and to draw his conclusions accordingly. With the frequent use of poll findings for political promotion, the admonition is particularly important.

☞ The Intensity of Feeling ☜

One other measurement that can be extremely important is the assessment of intensity of feeling. The direction of opinion may be overwhelmingly clear, but, then again, only a few people may care very much one way or the other.

As Lindsay Rogers simplistically but humorously mused twenty-two years ago:

I suppose a man who had been reading "Mr. Blandings Builds His Dream House," and who, in reply to the question: "Do you personally put much faith in the assurances that Stalin gives occasional visitors?" burst forth with: "Jesus H. Mahogany Christ, no!" would impress the most unperceptive interviewer as holding an opinion that was tolerably intense. Again, I suppose that to a question on military aid to the states of western Europe the reply: "I don't care a hoot in Hell," would suggest that the respondent had no decided feeling. But how about the nuances?[6]

Of course, these days, and even in his day, measuring intensity was not done by any such subjective assessment of tone of voice or inflection.

There are basically two methods of measuring intensity: one is to employ a numerical scale and the other is to state degrees of intensity. As to the first, after a person has stated an opinion, he can be shown, for example, a ten-point scale and told that the top of the scale represents the strongest opinion and the bottom of the scale represents the least strongly held opinion. The respondent would then be asked to select the position on the scale that best reflects the strength of his opinion. Such a numerical scale works best when checking the intensity of opinion with regard to political figures or institutions and must be used on issues with considerably more caution.

The verbal dimensions of intensity can be handled in many

125

different terms: Do you strongly agree, mildly agree, mildly disagree, or strongly disagree?, or Are you quite definite about your feeling or not at all definite? One of the most used and least effective methods of measuring intensity of feeling is to follow the substantive question with: "How strongly do you feel about this?" offering a list of degrees of intensity.

An ingenious technique we learned about from Archibald Crossley, the master of questioning technique, is a series of questions focused on a candidate or an issue which he calls "negative challenges". For example, would the respondent not be likely to change his mind or will he continue to feel as he does? Would the respondent not feel the other alternative might not work out almost as well? Does the respondent really feel it makes much difference which alternative is followed or not? And, are there any circumstances the respondent can imagine under which he might change his mind on the matter?

Thus, after these answers are scored and then scaled, Professor Rogers has been provided all the nuances of intensity he could ever ask for without, for example, needing to depend upon voice inflection. But, alas, there is not sufficient space on a questionnaire to go through such a battery of intensity questions for each candidate and on each issue.

Another approach is to uncover the division of opinion on an issue and then determine the likelihood of influencing a person's vote by taking a stand on the same issue. For instance, before the more lenient abortion law went into effect in New York State early in 1970, opinion divided two-to-one in favor of the new legislation. But, at the same time, only four-in-ten would have been influenced to vote one way or the other when a candidate took a stand on it. Thus, sentiment was overwhelmingly in favor, while the intensity of that sentiment was relatively slight in terms of affecting a respondent's support of a candidate. Two years later the situation had changed. The division of opinion in favor of the abortion law was narrowed while there was an increase in the number of people who felt strongly enough to be influenced one way or another when a candidate took a stand on the issue.

☞ Presidential Popularity: What Does It Mean? ☜

Second only to the preelection surveys, the frequently reported Presidential "popularity" figures are the most followed of all poll results. A President's disposition can vary in direct proportion to them. A drop of one or two percentage points can cause the greatest consternation in the White House and send staffers scurrying for an accounting of the decline. It little soothes the nerves of these staffers to report that a margin of three percentage points must be allowed in these ratings to account for probable sampling error since there were 1,500 interviews conducted. Bad ratings are bad press, and that is sufficient cause for worry.

Both Gallup and Harris regularly report the answers to their popularity questions. Gallup asks people whether they "approve or disapprove of the way Nixon is handling his job as President." Harris poses the question somewhat differently: "How would you rate the job Richard Nixon has been doing as President—excellent, pretty good, only fair, or poor?"

These "popularity" ratings are clearly a barometer. The question is, What are they a barometer of? The natural tendency for the ratings is to go down. This has been seen in the case of every President since Truman. When Truman came into office in 1945, the Gallup Poll showed him with an 87 percent approval rating. By October of the next year, the rating was down to 32 percent favorable. It bobbed up and down thereafter. Dwight Eisenhower had a 68 percent approval rating upon coming into office in 1953, which stayed around the 70 percent mark until the end of 1957, when it fell towards 60 percent and 55 percent. It never really recovered its earlier heights. John Kennedy's early ratings were in the low 70 percent range and dropped to 59 percent just prior to his assassination. Lyndon Johnson, coming in at a time of crisis, was buoyed up by early ratings of 79 percent and 80 percent, but by 1966 they had dropped to the 50's, and by the time the 1968 election came along they were in the low 40's. President Nixon has never had the advantage of such a high starting point (59 percent in January 1969) and his ratings have tended toward the 60 percent figure up to the spring of 1971, when they fell below the 50 percent mark for the first time.

These popularity ratings are boosted up from time to time, primarily in response to some decisive action taken by the President. After the Bay of Pigs fiasco, for example, President Kennedy's approval rating rose from 72 percent to 83 percent, according to the Gallup Poll. After the Cuban Missile Crisis, it rose 12 percentage points from 62 percent to 74 percent. Similarly, President Johnson's approval rating prior to the landing of American troops in the Dominican Republic was 64 percent, and afterwards it rose to 70 percent. Or, again, after the bombing of oil depots near Hanoi and Haiphong, his rating rose from 50 percent approval to 56 percent.

What this suggests is that the popularity ratings are a barometer of the extent to which the public perceives the President as taking decisive action with respect to a major national problem —particularly on the international scene. The ratings then tend to drop when it becomes clear to the public that some initiative has not worked, and they continue to do so until the next dramatic move. What influence, if any, these ratings have within the inner circles of the White House on matters of policy is hard to determine. It is hoped, however, that their impact is minimal. It is sobering to remember that seven months before his surprising upset of Thomas Dewey, Harry Truman's approval rating stood at a low 34 percent!

In our view, these popularity ratings represent little more than an artifact of the polling technique created in response to journalistic interest, and they certainly are not meaningful for guidance at the Presidential level.

☞ The Information Base of an Opinion ☜

In 1964 it was found that 62 percent of the American people did not know that the Soviet Union was *not* a member of NATO. Eighty-six percent of the public did not know who Sukarno was, and only 40 percent could correctly identify U Thant.[7] It is findings like these that lead the skeptic to ask how any credence can be put in polls which purport to report the public's view on important substantive issues.

This recurring dilemma was highlighted in a survey in one of the large eastern industrial states which asked people if they knew what "the so-called right-to-work law means." Only one in five knew the correct meaning, two in five gave incorrect answers, and the remainder said flatly that they did not know. (See Table 6–6.) When a follow-up question was asked as to whether people "favor or oppose" the right-to-work law, those respondents who knew what the law was were much less favorably disposed toward it than those who had incorrectly defined it. (See Table 6–7.)

Even though many respondents may not have all the information they think they have, the experienced researcher will be sensitive to the extent of the public's knowledge and take steps to provide as much information in intelligible terms as possible in the questions he asks.

People close to the national debate—journalists, politicians,

TABLE 6-6

Knowledge of "Right-to-Work" Law

		PERCENT
Correct:	The right to refuse to join a union when taking a job where a union exists	20%
Incorrect:	The right to be hired regardless of race, color, or creed	15
	The right to be hired in general (no mention of conditions)	20
	The requirement to join a union	2
	Something to do with unions	1
	Miscellaneous	1
Don't Know		41

(The five "Incorrect" responses — 15, 20, 2, 1, 1 — are bracketed together as 39.)

TABLE 6-7

Knowledge vs. Opinion on Right-to-Work Law

THE VIEWS OF THOSE WHOSE DEFINITION OF THE RIGHT-TO-WORK LAW WAS:	PERCENT FAVORING AND OPPOSING RIGHT-TO-WORK LAW		
	FAVOR	OPPOSE	NO OPINION
Correct	51	23	26
Incorrect	74	10	16

bureaucrats—tend to communicate with one another in a kind of short-hand language. There is a body of common terminology and an overall frame of reference with which national issues are discussed—"search and destroy," "Phase Two," no-knock provision," etc. Thus the easy assumption is often made that the

130

public understands the issues, and understands them in the same terms of reference.

When some major event brings an issue home to the public, opinions can be more readily sought as to the details and implications of contending positions on an issue. Thus, prior to President Nixon's announcements regarding "wage and price controls," the public's understanding was probably not adequate to have asked whether controls were favored or opposed. Afterwards, however, when the phrase became increasingly commonplace, the public's view could have been sought in a meaningful way. However, then there would be the tendency to err again, assuming that since "wage and price controls" was a phrase that had entered the public vocabulary questions could then go on to probe the public's view of "Phase Two."

This all does not mean that public opinion on complex national issues cannot be measured. When an issue is explained in some detail, people can generally give a thoughtful answer. Using a one or two sentence preamble before actually posing the question will usually suffice. The difficulty is to explain an issue clearly and fairly without boring or confusing the respondent.

With the advent of television, of course, the public is more informed. However, even those areas in which public knowledge is lacking are susceptible to worthwhile opinion research, even if only to discover basic concerns and possible lack of realism as to the public's view of the dimensions of problems confronting the nation.

☞ What It Means to Have "No Opinion" ☜

When a respondent is genuinely unable to answer a question, the finding is as important as determining his choice between response alternatives. Thus, "no opinion" percentages are important in their own right.

The "no opinion" reply can be brought about in three ways. It can be the wording of the question that puts the respondent off, either by failing to be readily understandable or by loading things one way or the other. Or, it can be occasioned by a reluctance of the respondent to commit himself for one reason or another; he may lack confidence in his ability to answer, or he may simply lack the knowledge required for reply. A third meaning for "no opinion" is, of course, that the individual, though knowledgeable, is genuinely undecided about the issue in question. Usually, with careful pretesting of a questionnaire, deficiencies can be overcome, and the tendency for people to refuse to verbalize an opinion is minimized.

When poll findings are reported, inclusion of the percentages for "no opinion" can be crucial to the analysis because they influence the percentages reported on the remaining response alternatives. For example, a Gallup Poll in late October 1971 asked people whether they felt "the United Nations organization is doing a good job or a poor job in trying to solve some of the problems it has to face." As might be expected, the "no opinion" percentage was appreciably lower for those with a college education than for those with grade or high school educations. (See Table 6–8.) Among the college educated, there were more percentage points remaining that could fall to the "good" or "poor" alternatives. It would be misleading to emphasize in a report the 54 percent of the college educated selecting "poor" compared to only 40 percent of the grade school educated, when nearly as many of the grade school educated had no opinion

(29 percent) as selected the "good" alternative (31 percent). When the percentages of people with "no opinion" are so varied, ignoring these differences can lead to spurious conclusions.

In political survey work, when questions pit one candidate against another, the "no opinion" or "undecided" percentages are very important. Their fluctuation is often a bellwether to changing loyalties, since people tend to go through an undecided phase in the process of shifting from one man to another.

TABLE 6-8

Attitude about U.N. Performance
(by education)

	PERCENT RATING U.N.'S PERFORMANCE AS:		
	GOOD	POOR	NO OPINION
College educated	33	54	13
High school educated	37	41	22
Grade school educated	31	40	29

The undecided percentage on candidate choice questions should seldom get much higher than 15 percent or 20 percent— usually less than 10 percent. If it is any higher, the candidate choice question probably has not been asked most effectively. Frequently, privately commissioned polls are leaked to the press showing extremely high undecided figures to bolster the claim that an unpromising electoral situation is still fluid and that "anything can happen." Most often, however, such leaks are a smokescreen to hide the poor showing of the client candidate.

Candidate choice questions that are too loosely worded tend to yield inflated undecided percentages. Experience teaches two things about candidate choice questions. The first is that the question should be as easy to answer as possible. Therefore, rather than ask people how they will "vote on election day in November," ask them "who they would most like to see win were the election being held *today*." Second, when a respondent says he is not sure whom he would like to see win, a follow-up question can be asked about which candidate he "leans toward as of now." The use of this second question usually reduces the initial undecided percentage by about half.[8]

In its final preelection survey, the Gallup Poll employs a special technique known as "the secret ballot." Rather than answering verbally, respondents are given a card on which are listed the names of the major parties and the candidates running for each party. The respondent is asked to check his preference on the card, fold it, and place it in a cardboard box the interviewer carries with him. In this way the undecided figure is reduced even further.[9]

These are some of the problems of interpretation that confront the survey researcher daily. It is hoped that their elucidation here will help those who look to the polls for a sense of the public mood.

These considerations of judgment and interpretation contain in them some implicit assumptions about the importance of public opinion. Therefore, the survey technique is employed to measure it. Drawing upon the material from preceding chapters, we now turn to a general discussion of what difference public opinion makes and the role of polling in a free society.

Notes

1. Letter to Edward Carrington, May 1, 1796, in *Writings of George Washington,* ed. John C. Fitzpatrick (Washington, D.C.: U.S. Government Printing Office, 1931–1944), vol. 35, p. 31.

2. *The New York Times,* November 14, 1971.

3. See Albert H. Cantril and Charles W. Roll, Jr., *Hopes and Fears of the American People* (New York: Universe Books, 1971); Hadley Cantril, *The Pattern of Human Concerns* (New Brunswick: Rutgers University Press, 1965); and Lloyd A. Free and Hadley Cantril, *The Political Beliefs of Americans* (New Brunswick: Rutgers University Press, 1967).

4. Free and Cantril, *Political Beliefs,* Chapter 3.

5. Ibid., p. 40.

6. Lindsay Rogers, *The Pollsters* (New York: A. A. Knopf, 1949), pp. 48–49.

7. Free and Cantril, *Political Beliefs,* p. 199.

8. Paul K. Perry, "Election Survey Procedures of the Gallup Poll," *Public Opinion Quarterly* 24 (Fall 1960): 538–539.

9. Ibid., pp. 541–542.

7

Public Opinion Polling In a Free Society

> Public opinion polls are useful if a politician uses them only to learn approximately what the people are thinking, so that he can talk to them more intelligently. The politician who sways with the polls is not worth his pay.
>
> RICHARD NIXON

"NOTHING is more dangerous than to live in the temperamental atmosphere of a Gallup Poll, always taking one's temperature. . . . There is only one duty, only one safe course, and that is to be right and not to fear to do or say what you believe to be right."[1] With this injunction Winston Churchill raised in contemporary form the oldest question perplexing the democratic form of government: What is the appropriate role and place of public opinion in determining the course of affairs?

Survey research, with its increasingly refined techniques measuring the public sentiment at any point in time on any set of issues, lends to public opinion a vividness and concreteness that did not exist before the advent of the polling art. Now poll results are everywhere, constantly reminding us that public opinion does exist and in a rather specific sense.

👉 The Place of Public Opinion 👈

The question is often asked about the circumstances under which political leaders should follow, lead, educate, cajole, or simply ignore public opinion. The issue is certainly not new, and while polling techniques have not raised any fundamentally new questions about the role of public opinion, they have indeed forced to the surface some of the traditional questions.

There were two points of view—each with its roots deep in European political tradition—which quickly emerged as the Founding Fathers framed our basic political institutions. One school of thought held that the determination of what was in the public interest could not be left to the people. They were held to be too ill-informed and too susceptible to momentary whims of passion to play a decisive role. This view was to be contrasted to the philosophy that the only legitimate source of judgment on major issues was to be found in the will of the people. The dilemma thus posed in these contending views was whether the nation's leaders were supposed to be responsible for the public's interest or to be responsive to the public's desires.

The former view was advocated most strongly by Alexander Hamilton. In urging the ratification of the U.S. Constitution, he took a cool view toward what role public opinion should play:

The republican principle demands that the deliberate sense of the community should govern the conduct of those to whom they intrust the management of their affairs; but it does not require an unqualified compliance to every sudden breeze of passion, or to every transient impulse which the people may receive from the arts of men, who flatter their prejudices to betray their interests. . . . When occasions present themselves, in which the interests of the people are at variance with their inclinations, it is the duty of the persons whom they have appointed to be guardians of those interests to withstand the temporary delusion, in order to give them time and opportunity for more cool and sedate reflection.[2]

In this he reflected almost literally the views of Edmund Burke, a member of the British Parliament. Writing to his Bristol constituents in 1774, Burke stated the classical case for a representative arriving at his own judgments completely independent of what his constituents want:

[A representative's] unbiased opinion, his mature judgment, his enlightened conscience, he ought not to sacrifice to you; to any man, or to any set of men living. These he does not derive from your pleasure; no, nor from the law and the constitution. They are a trust from Providence, for the abuse of which he is deeply answerable. Your representative owes you, not his industry only, but his judgment; and he betrays, instead of serving you, if he sacrifices it to your opinion.[3]

As for American governmental organization based on this line of thought, *The Federalist Papers* supported a U.S. Senate, with its staggered terms of six years and the then system of indirect elections by the various state legislatures, as "an institution [which] may be sometimes necessary as a defence to the people against their own temporary errors and delusions."[4] There was, however, to be one instrument of the Federal government to feel the effects of "transient public passions." "As it is essential to liberty that the government in general should have a common interest with the people, so it is particularly essential," says *The Federalist,* that the U.S. House of Representatives, elected for two year terms, "should have an immediate dependence on, and an intimate sympathy with, the people."[5]

Nearly fifty years later, a now-famous French observer of the American scene, Alexis de Tocqueville, warned:

A proceeding which will in the end set all the guarantees of representative government at naught is becoming more and more general in the United States; it frequently happens that the electors, who choose a delegate, point out a certain line of conduct to him, and impose a certain number of positive obligations which he is pledged to fulfill.[6]

Because most every American schoolboy is assigned readings from *The Federalist Papers* and from de Tocqueville's *Democ-*

racy in America, the burden of attention has been paid to the importance of the elected official remaining somewhat aloof from the views of his constituents. However, there are equally respectable representatives of the opposing view—the one that has become the target of so many observers since survey research has come upon the scene.

Twelve years before Burke declared his parliamentary independence from his Bristol constituents, Jean Jacques Rousseau wrote a treatise on civil government, *The Social Contract,* in which he described as the "general will" that sense of common interest which people recognize as something different from their selfish private interests and which must be the source of all sovereign power of a state. In pursuance of this general will:

The deputies of the people . . . are not and cannot be their representatives; they can only be their commissioners, and as such they are not qualified to conclude anything definitely. No act of theirs can be a law, unless it has been ratified by the people in person; and without that ratification nothing is a law.[7]

Recognizing that representatives often develop special interests that can be quite separate from those of the community at large, Rousseau, with Burke or Burke's philosophical predecessors in mind, gloats:

The people of England deceive themselves when they fancy they are free; they are so, in fact, only during the election of members of parliament; for as soon as a new one is elected, they are again in chains, and are nothing. And thus, by the use they make of their brief moments of liberty, they deserve to lose it.[8]

Thomas Jefferson, the author of our own Declaration of Independence from the monarchy of George III, saw it to be a "duty in those intrusted with the administration of [public] affairs to conform themselves to the decided choice of their constituents" because, as he said later, "it is rare that the public sentiment decides immorally or unwisely, and the individual who differs from it ought to distrust and examine well his opinion."[9]

Defining "republic" as "a government by its citizens in mass, acting directly and personally, according to rules established by the majority," Jefferson saw every other government as "more or less republican, in proportion as it has in its composition more or less of this ingredient of the direct action of the citizens."[10] Unlike Rousseau, recognizing such a pure republican form to be limited "to very narrow limits of space and population" hardly "practicable beyond the extent of a New England Township," Jefferson finds "the nearest approach to a pure republic, which is practicable on a large scale of country or population" to be "where the powers of the government, being divided, should be chosen by the citizens either *pro hac vice* [for one occasion only], or for such short terms as should render secure the duty of expressing the will of their constituents."[11]

The role of an elected official was clear to the young Abraham Lincoln. Seeking office in the Illinois legislature, he announced:

While acting as their [the people's] representative, I shall be governed by their will on all subjects upon which I have the means of knowing what their will is; and upon all others, I shall do what my own judgement teaches me will best advance their interests.[12]

In a speech in Congress, where he served as a Whig during the controversial Mexican War which was so vigorously supported by the Democratic Party, Lincoln scolded:

You [Democrats] violated the primary—the one great—living principle of all democratic representative government—the principle that the representative is bound to carry out the known will of his constituents . . . we hold the true republican position. In leaving the people's business in their hands, we cannot be wrong.[13]

There are several considerations which militate against the Rousseau-Jefferson-Lincoln point of view in today's world, however valid it may have been in an earlier day. For the Senator or Congressman there is the problem of precisely representing one's own constituents—all confined to a fractional area in the national entity—without taking into consideration the overall national interest. Thus, today, the installation of antiballistic missile sites may be an economic boon to the towns they are to be located near, but may prove detrimental to the nation. Or, conversely, they may be harmful to these towns but may prove vital to our national defense. The important consideration would have to be the national interest, not home town desires.

Rousseau's "general will" theories were to be operable only in small city states and Jefferson saw that the wider the geographical expanse for democratic rule, the further away from pure democracy democratic rule would be. Thus, what is good for South Boston, South Carolina, or South Dakota may not be good for the nation as a whole.

Recognizing the correct order of priorities, Burke warns his constituents:

You choose a member, indeed; but when you have chosen him, he is not a member of Bristol, but he is a member of PARLIAMENT. If the local constituent should have an interest or should form an hasty opinion evidently opposite to the real good of the rest of the community, the member for that place ought to be as far as any other from any endeavor to give it effect.[14]

Secondly, there is the problem of being caught up in the short range view of the mood of the public rather than the long term conception of a public interest which is not readily apparent. Completely relying upon the dictates of public opinion can have undesirable consequences for two reasons. In the words of Kenneth Janda, "voters' inclinations toward selfishness in promoting their own interests" and "their tendencies toward hasty and ill-considered actions" are factors which may lead "to unwise or unjust government policies."[15] It has been said that politicians only look ahead to the next election. If this is so, it might be also said that the people look ahead only to the next tax bill—which is usually an even more immediate occurrence. The emplacement of ABM missile sites may seem a sound defense tactic to the public, but the public is not likely to, nor might it be expected to, take into consideration how it appears to the world in general and to the U.S.S.R. in particular that this policy is adopted at the very time we are pursuing a disarmament line at the SALT talks.

Still a third problem arises. That is the increasing body of technical, scientific, or even merely general knowledge that is required before many of today's decisions can be soundly made. It is foolhardy to depend upon public opinion to tell us whether the installation of antiballistic missile sites across our northern states is a sound or an unsound defensive measure, a necessary or an unnecessary defensive step. Even on nontechnical subjects, the public cannot always be expected to have sufficient awareness of all the facts and enough understanding of the ramifications of these facts to produce sound guidance for their elected leaders.

Theodore Roosevelt clearly pointed the way for today's elected representative. Agreeing substantially with the Burke-Hamilton view, he said:

If on any point of real importance he finds that he conscientiously differs with them, he must, as a matter of course, follow his conscience, and thereby he may not only perform his highest duty, but also render the highest possible service to his constituents themselves.[16]

In the case of such a divergence occurring, Roosevelt adds that the elected official

. . . should not try to achieve his purpose by tricking his constituents or by adroitly seeking at the same time to thwart their wishes in secret and yet apparently to act so as to retain their good will.[17]

After declaring that, if the issue about which there is disagreement is of sufficient importance, the official "should be prepared to go out of office rather than surrender on a matter of vital principle," Roosevelt concludes:

Normally, however, he must remember that the very meaning of the word representative is that the constituents shall be represented. It is his duty to try to lead them to accept his views, and it is their duty to give him as large a latitude as possible in matters of conscience, realizing that the more conscientious a representative is the better he will in general represent them.[18]

Thus, Theodore Roosevelt was sensitive to the type of needs to which the later developed polling technique could respond. He sensed the importance of a leader honestly taking into account constituent views and, where they differ from his, using his leadership qualities to bring the people around, and, when this fails, at least developing a better understanding on their part of his action. The polling instrument is an important aid in helping to bring this all about.

☞ The Competence of Public Opinion ☜

The fundamental question raised by these conflicting strands of our political tradition basically is: What is the competence of public opinion? While this question calls for a philosophical answer, experience in the field of opinion research points up some of the considerations that should be borne in mind.

In our own view, the competence of public opinion is at the "feeling level." The public obviously cannot be expected to be informed and up-to-date in its understanding of complex issues, the implications of alternative courses of action, nor the advantages of specific instrumentalities by which a policy is effected. We agree with what Walter Lippmann wrote in 1925: ". . . when public opinion attempts to govern directly it is either a failure or a tyranny. It is not able to master the problem intellectually, nor to deal with it except by wholesale impact. . . . The intricate business of framing laws and administering them through several hundred thousand public officials is in no sense an act of the voters nor a translation of their will."[19]

However, when it comes to generalized impressions, in two areas the public's judgment usually proves sound and prophetic. The public is quick to spot a phony—the disingenuous politician who is facile and whose transparency soon betrays itself. The public is also very sensitive to the direction and adequacy of policies being pursued by its leaders. While public opinion takes longer to jell with regard to policies, once it becomes clear a policy is unworkable or simply getting too costly, the public will desert its leaders. As the late Professor Harwood Childs of Princeton University put it:

. . . the general public is especially competent, probably more competent than any other group—elitist, expert, or otherwise—to determine the basic ends of public policy, to choose top policy-makers, to appraise the results of public policy, and to say what, in the final analysis, is fair, just, and moral. On the other hand, the general public is not competent to determine the best means for attaining specific goals, to answer technical questions, to prescribe remedies for political, social and economic ills, and to deal with specialized issues far removed from the everyday experience and understanding of the people in general.[20]

Thus, in political research the crucial dimension from the public opinion standpoint is not whether people approve or disapprove of a given policy or the leader advocating a policy. Rather, it is the public's sense of trust and confidence in its leaders, when it comes to finding resourceful and effective ways of responding to problems. What it judges its leaders on, then, is less the substance of policies and programs than the overall impression of whether its leaders "are on top of things."

But Lippmann would argue in response: "The movement of opinion is slower than the movement of events. Because of that, the cycle of subjective sentiments on war and peace is usually out of gear with the cycle of objective developments. . . . The opinion deals with a situation which no longer exists."[21]

This forces a further differentiation regarding the public's competence to deal with matters of policy. We agree with Lippmann that the public cannot keep abreast of the twist and turn of events. But this does not mean that public opinion about these events is of political insignificance. When events or actions by leaders bring an issue home to the public, public opinion can quickly catch up to events, and when it does, it becomes all powerful. To quote Woodrow Wilson: "Opinion ultimately governs the world."[22] Opinion does not react to events unless they impinge in some meaningful way upon the level of basic individual concerns and individual self-interest.

Politicians often tend to exaggerate the degree to which the public pays attention to and cares about those procedural aspects of political life so important to them, e.g., the filibuster, seniority on Congressional committees, reapportionment, governmental organization, etc. However, on something less remote like school busing, which involves four sacred items to the American family—children, education, neighborhood, and the loss of hard-worked-for goals—the public's view sends politicians scurrying.

One major impact of television has been that it shortens the opinion lag to which Lippmann referred. TV undoubtedly helps hone the public's sensitivities to events and how its leaders are responding, and, also, it probably has helped the public become more alert to the difficulty of solving major problems. The medium has given the public a way to size up situations and individuals fairly quickly, and while the public's knowledge still lags behind the flow of events, TV will help keep current the public's impressions of the men at the helm and their policies, further cultivating its shrewdness of judgment.

Public opinion can be likened to a "system of dikes which channel public action or which fix a range of discretion within which government may act or within which debate at official levels may proceed."[23] This notion of the late V.O. Key "yields a different conception of the place of public opinion than does the notion of a government by public opinion in which, by some mysterious means, a referendum occurs on every major issue." With the dike concept:

The articulation between government and opinion is relatively loose. Parallelism between action and opinion tends not to be precise in matters of detail; it prevails rather with respect to broad purpose. And in the correlation of purpose and action, time lags may occur between the crystallization of a sense of mass purpose and its fulfillment in public opinion.[24]

The war in Indochina is the best single illustration of this concept. In a 1966 essay on public opinion about the war, Seymour Martin Lipset wrote: "To sum up the implications of the polls, it seems clear that the President holds the trump cards in dealing with the public on foreign policy matters. The public knows they do not know, and feel they must trust the President, for there is no one else on whom they can rely in the international field. . . . The President makes public opinion, he does not follow it. . . . The polls tell the President how good a politician he is."[25]

As events have since proven, Lipset greatly overstated the amount of latitude the President had. As Bill Moyers put it in an essay two years later:

It should be obvious that a President faces no quest more difficult than the search for an accurate reading of how far and how fast he can lead the people. As difficult as the task is, he must try. He must try because there are questions on which governments dare not act without evidence of genuine support. When policies and laws outdistance public opinion, or take public opinion for granted, or fail to command respect in the conscience of the people, they lose their "natural" legitimacy. . . . Vietnam has proven that good intentions on the part of a nation's leaders will not substitute for the conscious involvement of the people in the decision to go to war.[26]

History is replete with other instances which highlight the crucial role played by public opinion. For example, juxtapose the situations of Leon Blum of France and Franklin Roosevelt. Both faced the same dilemma—how to mobilize their nation for possible involvement in war when public opinion was not ready to take the step. Blum, upon assuming the premiership of the Popular Front Government in 1938, became aware of the urgent need for France to beef up its defenses. Yet public opinion was completely unprepared. Blum and his defense program had no chance of success and both were defeated in the resistant upper house of the French legislature.[27] And what came after was too little and too late.

President Roosevelt, sensitive to the need to carry public sentiment with him, had the benefit of repeated soundings of public opinion undertaken for him by Hadley Cantril from 1939 on. As Cantril recounted the period later:

The trend shown . . . [see Figure 7–1] indicates the uncanny way in which the President was able to balance public opinion around his policies. The precise question asked was . . . one of those the President said he hoped could be repeated at frequent intervals: "So far as you personally are concerned, do you think President Roosevelt has gone too far in his policies of helping Britain, or not far enough?" In spite of the fact that United States aid to Britain constantly increased after May of 1941, the proportion of people who thought the President had gone too far, about right, or not far enough remained fairly constant. This was precisely the situation he wanted to maintain during these critical months; hence his eagerness to learn the results of our periodic soundings.[28]

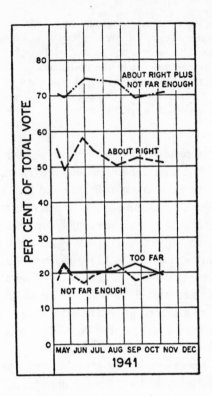

FIGURE 7–1

Two other episodes portray the dire consequences when the nation's leaders misread the state of public opinion. Only once in our nation's history did the process of civil government break down—the Civil War. A reading of the first volume of Bruce Catton's centennial history of that war, *The Coming Fury,* makes abundantly clear the misguided optimism of the political leadership both in the North and in the South just prior to the attack on Fort Sumter which touched off that war. Much of the South did not believe that Lincoln and his administration truly spoke the views of the North. The people of the North, it was felt, would never follow this "abolitionist" Lincoln faction into an undesirable war merely to force their Southern brethren to remain in a Union of states the South did not want; therefore, even if war came, the North would be unable to field a large Army.

On the other hand, Northern leadership assumed the people of the South would, in general, remain loyal to the Union. Lincoln probably grossly overestimated the amount of Unionist sentiment in Virginia and other border states. He took false hope from the fact that "even in Mississippi and Alabama, there were men who argued boldly and with some public support against secession."[29] He failed to understand that Southern pro-Union sentiment was purely conditional—only existing as long as no strain was put upon it, but when a real test came it would fall apart. Since "state's claims ran deeper" than Union claims, denouncers of treason—even in Mississippi and Alabama—would follow their state's banner even into treason.

These erroneous assumptions on both sides—optimistic in a self-deceiving way—did not prevent ill-considered and irreversible actions which eventually led to war in the early months of 1861. The momentous actions based on these assumptions were the attack on Fort Sumter by the South and the proclamation by Lincoln levying soldiers from each state. The three infantry regiments requested of Virginia to coerce her sister states back into the Union made it impossible for the "Old Dominion" herself to avoid secession. It is clear that sounder decisions would have resulted on both sides if survey data showing general Northern support of the Lincoln position had been available to the South and if accurate polling information indicating the great likelihood of general Southern support of secession once the North used coercion had been available to Lincoln and his advisors.

It might be argued by historians that this war had to be fought and had to be won by the North in order to bring about fulfillment of American ideals. It also might be argued, however, that, enlightened by accurate attitudinal intelligence about the other side, leadership on both sides might have brought about peaceful fulfillment of American ideals. At the very least, the eventual victor might have accomplished the same result in a shorter, less bloody period had greater care been taken to keep Virginia from joining the Confederacy. As Lincoln himself admitted later: "I claim not to have controlled events, but confess plainly that events have controlled me."[30]

A more contemporary misjudgment of where public opinion stood is found in the Bay of Pigs fiasco of the Eisenhower and Kennedy Administrations. During April and May 1960, Lloyd A. Free conducted an opinion survey in Cuba for the Institute for International Social Research. This was not an insignificant feat since Castro had been in power for a little more than a year. A report was prepared based upon 1,000 carefully executed interviews in Havana and other urban areas throughout Cuba—where about 60 percent of the Cuban people live. The report showed that far from despair, the Cuban people backed Castro overwhelmingly, were enthused about the revolution Castro had brought to Cuba, were relieved that the days of Batista were over, and were optimistic about the future of the country.[31]

Free's report was published in July 1960 and made available publicly to the governmental and scholarly communities. A story of the report's findings appeared in *The New York Times* on August 2 and considerable interest was shown in it. Nonetheless, in the transitional days between the Eisenhower and Kennedy Administrations the report got buried and forgotten. It surfaced only after the ill-fated invasion attempt. When it was later learned that the report's findings directly contradicted the assumption of the invasion—that the Cuban populace would join the handful of invaders in an overthrow of the Castro regime—Arthur Schlesinger wrote poignantly that he only wished a copy had come to his attention earlier. The tragedy here was that the research tool, which by this time had established itself even in the international area, was disregarded.

☞ Leadership of Opinion ☜

There is a tendency for people in positions of high leadership to develop an unbridled confidence in their own judgment. They have by and large survived political risks and made some basically sound calculations with regard to what is on the public's mind. Thus, they feel more competent than others to look over situations and make their own determinations as to what the state of public thinking is on an issue.

There is, therefore, an accompanying tendency for leaders to act quickly on the assumption that they have carefully weighed public opinion considerations. Decisions are announced or actions taken which often leave the public cold or in some instances spark outright opposition.

Three factors militate against sensitivity to the public opinion dimension of problems even on the part of seasoned political leaders. First, by definition political decisions are made amid great ambiguity. The choices are never easy. The alternatives are seldom clearly cut and they are often equally unattractive. In the words of the British Tory leader, Sir Gerald Nabarro, party politics is "the art of advocating something you know to be bad, as the only alternative to something you know to be a great deal worse."[32] The information available conflicts, special interests collide and staffers vie for the decision-maker's attention. The result is that subtle forces are at work to provide ways of reducing the ambiguity. In the extreme case, simplistic notions of what the relevant constituency consists of are propounded. Assumptions are made about "the silent majority," "the black vote," "youth," etc., as though these population groups can be thought of as segments of the population having an internal consistency of view.

This temptation is fed by a second factor we have touched upon earlier. This is the shared terms of reference with which national policies and priorities are debated. Politicians, journalists, bureaucrats and the panoply of consultants-researchers-observers all tend to employ similar abstractions, words and information sources when commenting on the political scene. As the circle closes there are often mistaken assumptions made as to the state of public opinion.

Closely allied is a third factor, which is the frequently manifested cynicism of political leaders as to how suggestible the public is. It is often assumed that speeches, dramatic gestures, or good TV coverage will produce short-term gains with the public. Obviously, the public is often impressed. But consider that, after all the exposure given President Nixon on his visit to the People's Republic of China, there was no meaningful increase in those feeling he was doing a good job as President.[33]

The task of responsible leadership is to resist these influences, uncover the bases of consensus and cultivate a sense of community. Or, as Henry Cabot Lodge phrased it:

. . . the interests which men have in common and which bind them together are more numerous and important than those which drive them apart. The cleverer (a politician) is at . . . divisive tactics, the more evil he is. Because a united people can overcome all obstacles, it is a public servant's job to find the common ground and to unite.[34]

In two principal respects, research into the state of public opinion can help. Research can help uncover the common ground amid the din of conflicting claims and help leaders find the bases for consensus. It can help elucidate the basic concerns of the people, place into context the topical issues of the moment and alert leaders to what it is in public opinion they had better pay attention to. As Lincoln put it: "What I want is to get done what the people desire to have done and the question for me is how to find that out exactly."[35]

At the other end of the process, research can provide a check on the claims of special interests which represent themselves as advocating the public interest. A superb example is found in the late 1940s. In 1947 the Republican Congress passed, over President Truman's veto, the Taft-Hartley Act with its strict regulation of organized labor. Truman, with the backing of labor leaders, attacked the law vigorously in the 1948 Presidential campaign and promised its repeal.

With Truman's surprise victory, Taft-Hartley appeared doomed. Robert Taft, up for reelection in 1950, looked to all equally doomed because of Ohio's large labor vote. However, a national poll was taken by the late Claude Robinson in early 1949 which showed that while two-thirds (69 percent) of labor union members did not "think that Congress should have passed this bill," overwhelming majorities approved of virtually every major provision of the bill when questioned about each separately. Armed with this knowledge, Taft carried his campaign right into union bailiwicks and confronted the issue head-on. Marked for sure defeat, Taft instead carried every industrial county in Ohio and defeated his popular challenger in a landslide with 57.5 percent of the vote.[36]

In our view this all suggests that opinion research—technically competent and sensitive to existing political realities—can enhance the strength of the democratic process by improving communication between the leader and the led. On the one hand, regular opinion soundings provide yet another way for the public's view to become known—particularly between elections. Were it not for the polls, President Johnson and others would not have known how profound the disaffection of the American people was with the war in Vietnam. In the absence of poll findings it would have been easier to dismiss the peace sentiment in the country as representing a few disenchanted and misdirected "peaceniks" and "doves."

On the other hand, insights obtained through opinion research can help alert leaders to stresses in their relationship with the public and uncover the sources of these stresses before it is too late. Research can thus contribute greatly to the stability of the political process.

With the speed and complexity of modern life these communication linkages are all the more important because it is all the more imperative that political leaders and the public understand one another. With the advent of opinion research it has been possible to reduce the time required for this transfer to take place. It is also now possible to remove much of the guesswork as regards how far ahead of or behind the public the nation's leaders are.

Opinion research can contribute in a number of specific areas:

1. Research can uncover areas of public ignorance, misunderstanding and indifference. At a time in which the Johnson Administration was making some basic calculations with respect to U.S. policy in Southeast Asia, the finding of the Michigan Survey Research Center that one-fourth of the American public did not even know mainland China was ruled by a communist regime could have been of the utmost importance.[37]

2. The public often does not understand how specific actions or policies relate to long-term objectives. Research can highlight these areas of confusion and help leaders then convey to the public what some of the considerations are that have been taken into account in the formulation of policies and why they show promise of being effective.

3. The public is usually ill-prepared for unexpected contingencies. Research that uncovers ignorance or indifference among the public can alert leaders to the need for preparing the public for eventualities that may lie ahead.

4. Conversely, the public may, in certain instances, have unrealistic expectations of what will follow from some action. We noted earlier how the popularity figures of Presidents tend to soar after periods of decisive Presidential initiatives. However, in all cases the luster soon vanishes as it becomes clear the action has not solved the problem of the moment.

To put it another way, the task of leadership, as far as public opinion is concerned, consists of a number of elements. Serious research systematically injected at the highest levels can help leaders maximize their leadership potential in helping to:

1. provide and articulate the context within which specific actions are taken and instrumentalities relied upon;
2. provide perspectives on the future alerting the public to difficulties likely to be encountered and building an opinion base for policies that are judged necessary over the long term;
3. specify the relationship between tactical considerations and overall policy objectives;
4. communicate the bases for judgment; and
5. reaffirm basic values in times of crisis and periods of rapid change.

☞ Polls and the Public Trust ☜

This all means that the public opinion research community has taken unto itself an immense public trust. With each successive preelection survey that comes close to the mark, the reputation of the profession will be enhanced. Since in the public mind one poll tends to equal another, the good firms will carry the not-so-good with them as people increasingly will feel "the polls" are something that ought to be taken seriously.

There are a number of dimensions of this public trust which the responsible research organization keeps in mind. The foremost is integrity—the integrity of the research and the integrity of the relationship with the client. The reader will recall some illustrations in the first chapter of rather flagrant abuse by pollsters of their client's confidence.

A second dimension is technical proficiency. Before campaigns research firms descend like locusts upon candidates and private interests, all eager to obtain their own reading of the political situation. Many firms are new, springing up locally or spinning off from established organizations. The usual process is that a candidate's staff is approached by several competing research firms. Seldom is there sufficient depth of knowledge about polling on the part of the candidate or his staff to judge the good from the bad. Often an artificial sense of precision is conveyed by a research firm which claims that it can exactly measure and quantify all the political mysteries and intangibles which perplex candidates daily.

The selling points that carry the day thus often have little to do with the quality of research that will be delivered. Candidates are almost always impressed by the previous clients a polling firm has worked for. Flattery and inside-dopesterism often pique a candidate's interest. Also, cost considerations are frequently decisive. In the research profession, while there are rare exceptions, the best salesmen do not make the best researchers and the best researchers are poor salesmen.

What is sacrificed in terms of quality is problematical—and frequently not demonstrable to the client uninitiated in survey technique. However, in survey research, as in all else, one gets only what is paid for. Sampling procedures are complex, involving a myriad of details. Interviewing costs inflate at a rate of 7 to 10 percent a year. Tailoring survey design to each client's unique situation and needs takes the time of experts.

A third dimension of the public trust applies primarily to the larger nationally syndicated polls. Their clientele are not the larger nationally syndicated polls. Their clientele are not the politicians but the news media and, therefore, the public at large. A number of specific obligations follow.

Now that the public has become more knowledgeable about the interpretation of poll data, more comprehensive analyses and presentations in the published releases of the syndicated polls are overdue. The cosmetic questions of Presidential popularity, candidate standings, and public issue questions presented in oversimplified form will hopefully recede, giving way to more subtle and discriminating analyses in depth. In this way the frequent incongruities of public opinion can be explained and accounted for without it becoming necessary for the researcher to engage in political commentary.

One important function the published polls can serve is to provide the public-at-large with a greater appreciation of its own attitudinal make-up. That is, the layman who reads poll findings will learn more about how his own view on the issues of the day differ from the country at large and particular segments of the population. This kind of interchange can help improve understanding—if not communication—between people in a nation as diversified and heterogeneous as ours.

One danger is that national poll results may give a false impression of majority sentiment on major issues. This can happen when an insufficient number of questions are employed to ferret out facets of opinion on complex issues. Given the interest in the national polls by political leaders, the erroneous impression of where the majority stands on issues makes it easy for leaders to find seductive reassurance in limited surface data they find compatible, without delving in depth into the complexities of the problem.

The polls have a major impact, too, in their reports of opinion in nonelection situations. The public debate about U.S. policies in Indochina has often been filled with citations of what "the polls showed." As we have noted, the polls did serve the democratic process well by helping to articulate the public's growing unease about developments in Southeast Asia. But the responsibility was immense. Percentages have a way of becoming realities in their own right. In the heat of debate it is useless to point out that the expected sampling error must be taken into account or that a question with a specific wording affected the results.

The most effective syndicated polls will have to be closely attuned to existing political realities. Questions which pose completely unrealistic policy alternatives are as meaningless or misleading as those which present alternatives so loaded that no credence can be placed in the responses to them. So long as the syndicated polls are part of the journalistic world, both the pollster and the press have responsibilities of honoring the public trust.

☞ Policing the Polls? ☜

For years, there has been discussion of policing and monitoring the public opinion research business. The polling profession itself, through the American Association for Public Opinion Research (AAPOR), has taken the initiative. In 1968, it adopted a code of professional ethics dealing with public disclosure of procedures followed in surveys.[38]

Another approach has been attempted by members of Congress and state legislatures by way of regulatory legislation. In 1968, legislation was introduced in the Congress aimed at requiring the disclosure of procedures employed in surveys intended for public dissemination. It provided that this information be filed with the Librarian of Congress within 3 days after the release of poll results, with a possible penalty of 90 days in prison for failure to comply. (It was reintroduced in 1971 as H.R. 5003.)

A second attempt in Congress was the proposal of Senator Charles Goodell in December 1970 (just after his defeat for reelection) to allow a civil action to be brought against any person who released a private survey and failed to disclose the procedures employed. If the sponsor of the survey did not know what procedures had been employed, the action could then be brought against the research organization.

Suggestions in this direction overlook a number of important considerations. First of all, constitutional questions of freedom of speech and freedom of the press most certainly would arise as the problem looms of differentiating between systematic attitude research and impressionistic political reporting about opinion (such as the inquiring reporter interviews with the man-in-the-street). As George Gallup has written:

> To avoid conflict with the constitutional right of free speech and of a free press, Congress and the courts would have a nigh impossible task of trying to draw a distinction between a purportedly systematic attempt to gauge sentiment, as opposed to one that might be employed by a political observer.[39]

Even were these constitutional issues to be resolved, there is serious question as to how regulatory procedures would be implemented. Where would the competence be marshaled to pass upon the quality of the research procedures that had been disclosed? Practitioners can hardly be expected to judge each other's work. Outsiders without practical experience are not qualified. As we have noted in earlier chapters, a balance must always be struck between the precision desired in a survey and the resources available to pay for it. Thus, the question arises when evaluating research procedures: How good is good? A further danger arises that the special interests which come to the surface with any governmental regulatory procedure would become involved and, with time, would broaden the scope of any regulation. This state of affairs would almost certainly ensure *sub rosa* polling arrangements because politicians will always need their own independent, confidential, and private sources of information.

When opinion research is of poor quality, through either inadvertent sloppiness or deliberate malintent, the person that suffers most is he who relies upon the research. Thus, it would seem to us that the mass media that publish polls intended for public dissemination would want to obtain from their research organization full disclosure of methods and procedures. So, too, in privately commissioned polls, both the candidate and the potential contributor will come out the loser when relying upon a poorly executed poll.

Clearly, it is not the polling community that must bear the burden alone. The most promising approach will be to further an understanding of polls on the part of politicians, the press, and the public. Much of the difficulty results from the widespread ignorance among the news media about the polls. Reporters of the political scene, ever anxious for information and dramatic figures around which to build tomorrow's story, are frequently taken in by "the polls." As one political aide put it: "The papers need to be educated very badly."

It is in response to this need that the National Council on Public Polls (NCPP) was set up. Upon the initiative of George Gallup and Archibald Crossley, NCPP was organized several years ago by principal polling firms. While NCPP's membership consists primarily of the pollsters, its interest is in trying to get the newspapers to adopt specific ground rules regarding how the polls are reported. With the flurry of leaked polls every election year, NCPP's intent is to ensure that sufficient context be provided in a newspaper's accounting of a poll to protect both journalist and pollster, as well as the public.

One of the most encouraging signs is the developing awareness, on the part of the newspapers and the broadcast industry, of the need to rationalize the reporting of poll findings. *The*

160

New York Times, which has traditionally been very careful about polls, has recently assigned one of its reporters to become the in-house expert. His job is to become sufficiently versed in polling techniques to provide *The Times* a resource for making its own determination of which polls should be reported and not reported. This involves developing enough perspective to be able to assess the many local polling organizations whose work surfaces during campaigns, as well as to check against the temptation to read more into opinion findings than exists.

Another useful development in the direction of public education would be fuller coverage of the survey technique and its applications in the college curriculum and even at the high school level.

To summarize, those advocating regulation of the polls seek to place the burden of accountability exclusively upon the polling profession. This is clearly absurd. But, to pursue the argument, there are serious constitutional questions that are bound to arise. At the same time, there is some danger that injury could be done to one of the major functions the polls serve in our political process, i.e., facilitation of the communication between leaders and led. In our view, the only sound alternative in bringing about the responsible execution, interpretation, and use of polls lies in the educational process.

☞ Looking Ahead ☜

As sound polling techniques become better understood and better appreciated, new uses and new developments can be expected to emerge.

On the political side, it is probable that candidates, incumbents, and party committees at the higher level will begin to develop their own survey research capabilities. It is probable that staff personnel will include people versed in polling techniques who can design, execute, and analyze a competent opinion survey. Such an approach could be based on contractual arrangements with independent interviewing agencies and data processing firms. This approach will provide research that is targeted more closely with the day-by-day information needs of the principal; it will ensure security and reduce costs considerably. It will facilitate something that is desperately needed: an annual opinion audit to keep Governors, U.S. Senators, and Congressmen abreast of constituent assessment of their leadership, as well as constituent expectations and concerns on broader subjects.

The major drawback of this development of staff-conducted surveys would be the difficulty of maintaining tough-minded objectivity so that the politicians' interests are served and not flattered. A second danger might be that these surveys would have the purpose of external use for fund raising and other promotional activities, rather than for internal guidance. This danger, however, would be defused, at least to some extent, by the publicly known fact that the survey had been conducted by a leader's own staff members—a factor which may well compel the use of surveys for "intelligence" rather than promotion.

One development that has already emerged is the establishment of consulting firms that specialize in telephone canvassing of voters to ascertain candidate and party preferences along with public issue priorities. This information, accompanied by basic population characteristics, is computerized, enabling a candidate to direct campaign mailings to potential supporters. With such a canvass, a candidate can make personalized appeals to specific individuals on the basis of their age, union affiliation, sense of priority on the issues, and so on. This practice is not usually done by polling organizations, an important ethic of which is to protect the anonymity of the person interviewed.

This canvassing practice has the disturbing dimension of

Orwell's *1984,* for is it not possible that the political propensities of all individual Americans of voting age could be stored in a computer beyond the reach of the public? But in an even more immediate sense, this kind of canvassing, followed by direct communication with the individual, will make it more difficult for opinion research firms to obtain their type of meaningful interviews where the anonymity of the respondent is protected.

Another general trend is the development by newspapers of their own polling operations with respect to sentiment in their own states or localities. For some time, such papers as *The Saint Petersburg Times, The Des Moines Register,* and *The Minneapolis Tribune* have conducted reputable scientific polls. Similarily, Joe Belden and Mervin Field have conducted regular polls which are supported by newspapers in their respective states, Texas and California.

The first newspaper chain to develop opinion survey capabilities is the Knight Newspapers. Philip Meyer of the *Miami Herald* has been assigned responsibility in this area, and he has developed an impressive understanding of the intricacies of the survey technique.

This is an encouraging trend leading toward better general understanding of what polls are all about. As these local polls become more prevalent, a yardstick against which to measure the performance of private polls in the area is provided.

Another possible development is public opinion research by the Federal Government on issues not directly related to government programs. At present, the government contracts much survey research out to private firms and also relies a good deal upon research of the Bureau of the Census that is not just of a head-counting nature. The time may come, however, when serious consideration will be given to providing the nation's leaders with a ready instrument for conducting more extensive attitude research through Federal facilities.

POLLS

There are a number of compelling reasons why such a development as the Federal Government establishing its own capability is not likely to serve the public interest. Above all, information is power and this kind of capability would make available to the incumbent administration a knowledge base not readily available to the opposition. It is impossible to conceive of any public opinion research on major national issues devoid of political and partisan overtones. Take, for instance, the survey in late 1971 regarding the public's attitude toward wage and price controls, which was conducted by the heretofore politically pure Bureau of the Census. The obvious danger is that government agencies whose purpose is to provide an objective monitoring of socio-economic-demographic trends will be compromised. The ultimate conclusion to this trend could be government manipulation of facts and figures—and eventually the information given the public. Another concern is that such a resource within the Federal Government could inflate the role of public opinion in matters of specific policy choices—areas in which the public is not competent in most instances.

With new communication technologies developing at so fast a pace, there will be attempts to exploit the polling technique to provide instant analysis of the mood of the people. In the regulations promulgated by the Federal Communications Commission regarding the development of cable TV, it was stipulated that a two-way capability be provided such that the viewer can communicate to a central point. This would make possible national referenda within a matter of minutes, thus inflating the role of public opinion. While such referenda might make for good TV programming, the thought boggles the mind that political pundits and second-guessers could discuss so major a message as the President's State of the Union Address, having instantly at their disposal yes-or-no answers from the public about many of the complex issues that had been raised.

This kind of instant referendum would tend to foster the

164

more superficial kinds of public opinion assessment and not provide the comprehensive analyses toward which the survey technique should be directed.[41]

There is no doubt that the survey technique will be used in many new ways. The danger will always persist that the polls will be employed to ease the way for leaders who pander to the people's prejudices and exploit their many legitimate fears. Also, there will continue to persist the pollster who abuses the public trust with simplistic characterizations of the state of opinion.

The responsibility for the survey research community is immense. But so, too, is the obligation of those who use, report and follow the polls so closely. Now that the polls have come of age, the public has a need to know more about them. The more the potentialities—and limitations—of the polling technique are understood, the greater is the likelihood that opinion research will be employed in a responsible and meaningful fashion. It is toward that end this book has been written.

We do not suggest that public opinion should be followed at every turn in decision making. We do suggest, however, that public opinion must be taken into account *before* decisions are made if there is to be any chance of their successful implementation. Far from constraining the options available to the decision-maker, reliable measurements of opinion can greatly enhance the range of choice and maneuver open to him. Without such insight, his initiatives can backfire or be misdirected as they collide with public misunderstanding, frustrations, resistances, and the many other barriers comprising the "system of dikes" to which V. O. Key referred.

It is not just a matter of finding in the polls a vivid and incisive device supportive of a kind of direct democracy. Rather, the polls can take the lead in helping the public and its leadership to understand one another better. For the more faithfully the public's view is ascertained and taken into account, the greater is the chance that decisions of those at the helm will be both right and enduring.

Notes

1. Quoted in Hadley Cantril, *The Human Dimension: Experiences in Policy Research,* (New Brunswick, N.J.: Rutgers University Press, 1967) p. 42.

2. *The Federalist,* no. 71, thought to have been written by Alexander Hamilton. This view was supported by George Washington: "The wishes of the people . . . may not entirely accord with our true policy and interest." John C. Fitzpatrick, ed., *Writings of George Washington* (Washington, D. C.: U. S. Government Printing Office, 1931–1944), Vol. II, p. 289.

3. In his letter to the Electors of Bristol, 1774.

4. *The Federalist,* no. 63, thought to have been written by Alexander Hamilton or James Madison.

5. *The Federalist,* no. 52, thought to have been written by Alexander Hamilton or James Madison.

6. Alexis de Tocqueville, *Democracy in America* (New York: Oxford University Press, 1947), pp. 156–157.

7. Jean Jacques Rousseau, *The Social Contract* (New York: Hafner Publishing Co., 1949), p. 85.

8. Ibid., p. 85.

9. In a letter to John Jay in *The Writings of Thomas Jefferson,* ed. P. L. Ford (New York: G. P. Putnam's Sons, 1896), Vol. 4, p. 89; and in a letter to William Findlay in *The Writings of Thomas Jefferson,* ed. P. L. Ford (New York: G. P. Putnam's Sons, 1896), Vol. 8, p. 27.

10. Letter from Thomas Jefferson to John Taylor, May 28, 1816, as quoted in *Writings,* ed. P. L. Ford, Vol. 10, pp. 27–31.

11. Ibid.

12. Lincoln to the editor, *Sangamo Journal* (June 13, 1836), quoted in *Lincoln's Complete Works,* ed. by John Nicolay and John Hay (New York: Francis D. Tandy, 1905), Vol. I, p. 15.

13. Speech in Congress, July 27, 1848, in *Lincoln's Complete Works,* ed. by John Nicolay and John Hay, Vol. I, p. 71 and Vol. II, p. 69.

14. In a speech to the Electors of Bristol, 1774, Edmund Burke, *Collected Works,* Vol. II, p. 96.

15. Kenneth Janda, "Representational Behavior," *International En-*

cyclopedia of the Social Sciences, ed. David L. Sills (New York: The Macmillan Co., 1968), Vol. 13, p. 475.

16. From an article in *Outlook* (January 21, 1911), quoted in *The Works of Theodore Roosevelt,* ed. Hermann Hagedorn, Memorial Edition, (New York: Charles Scribner's Sons, 1923–1926), Vol. XIX, p. 93.

17. Ibid.

18. Ibid., pp. 93–94.

19. Walter Lippmann, *The Phantom Public* (New York: Harcourt, Brace and Co., 1925), quoted in Clinton Rossiter and James Lare, *The Essential Lippmann* (New York: Random House, 1963), p. 110.

20. Harwood L. Childs, *Public Opinion: Nature, Formation and Role* (Princeton: Van Nostrand, 1965), p. 350.

21. Walter Lippmann, "Everybody's Business and Nobody's" from *Today and Tomorrow* (April 11, 1941), quoted in Rossiter and Lare, *Lippmann,* pp. 96–97.

22. Speech, April 20, 1915, quoted in *The Home Book of American Quotations,* ed. Bruce Bohle (New York: Dodd Mead and Co., 1967), p. 274.

23. V. O. Key, *Public Opinion and American Democracy* (New York: Knopf, 1964), p. 552.

24. Ibid., p. 553.

25. Seymour Martin Lipset, "The President, The Polls and Vietnam," *Transaction* 3, no. 6 (September–October, 1966): 24.

26. Bill D. Moyers, "One Thing We Learned," *Foreign Affairs* (July 1968): pp. 661–662. (Italics provided.)

27. In putting forth the defense measures he proposed, Blum pronounced that ". . . we shall prove that free peoples can rise to . . . their duties, that democracies are capable, through a voluntarily accepted discipline, of deploying strength that is not obtained elsewhere except through blind obedience." But because public opinion had not been readied effectively Blum failed to prove this point. See William L. Shirer, *The Collapse of the Third Republic* (New York: Simon and Schuster, 1969), pp. 336–337.

28. Hadley Cantril, *The Human Dimension: Experiences in Policy Research* (New Brunswick: Rutgers University Press, 1967), p. 50.

29. Bruce Catton, *The Coming Fury* (Garden City: Doubleday, 1961), p. 188.

30. Letter to A. G. Hodges, April 4, 1864. In *The Lincoln Encyclopedia,* ed. Archer H. Shaw (New York: Macmillan, 1950), p. 114.

31. Lloyd A. Free, *Attitudes of the Cuban People Toward the Castro Regime* (Princeton: Institute for International Social Research, July 1960); see also Hadley Cantril, *Human Dimension,* pp. 1–5.

32. Quoted in *The New York Times,* October 12, 1969, in The Week in Review section.

33. The Gallup Poll found in interviewing just after the President's trip (March 3–5, 1972) that 56 percent approved of the job he was doing. In results from interviews February 4–7, the figure was 53 percent.

34. Quoted in William J. Miller, *Henry Cabot Lodge* (New York: Heineman, 1967), p. 205.

35. As quoted in Hadley Cantril, "Public Opinion in Flux," *Annals of the American Academy of Political and Social Science* (March 1942): 136.

36. Letter from L. Richard Guylay, January 20, 1972; and, Opinion Research Corporation, "The Taft-Hartley Law and Its Successor," from *The Public Opinion Index for Industry,* Vol. VII, No. 2 (February 1949).

37. Reported in A. T. Steele, *The American People and China* (New York: McGraw-Hill, 1966).

38. Specifically, the following should be included in reports of survey findings made public: the population being surveyed, the size of the sample, how the sample was drawn, the exact wording of questions, the date of interviewing, and how the interviews were obtained.

39. George Gallup, *The Sophisticated Poll Watcher's Guide* (Princeton: Princeton Opinion Press, 1972), p. 196.

40. Childs, *Public Opinion,* p. 353.

41. For a discussion of the implications of cable TV for the political process see Ithiel de Sola Pool and Herbert E. Alexander, *Politics in a Wired Nation,* A Report Prepared for the Sloan Commission on Cable Communications (September 1971).

ACKNOWLEDGMENTS

We would like to thank the following organizations for permission to use quotations from their publications in this book:

"One Thing We Learned" by Bill D. Moyers, *Foreign Affairs* (July 1968): 661–662.

"Do Polls Help Democracy?" from *Time*, The Weekly Newsmagazine (May 31, 1968): 19; © Time, Inc.

Adlai Stevenson as quoted in *The Hidden Persuaders* by Vance Packard (New York: David McKay, 1957), p. 172. © 1957 by Vance Packard. Reprinted by permission of Collins-Knowlton-Wing.

Polls, Television and the New Politics by Harold Mendelsohn and Irving Crespi (Scranton, Pa.: Chandler Publishing Company, 1970), p. 165.

"Role of the Press in Presidential Politics," by Elmer Cornwell, Jr. in *Politics and the Press,* ed. Richard W. Lee (Washington, D. C.: Acropolis Books, 1970), p. 19.

The Pollsters by Lindsay Rogers (New York: Alfred A. Knopf, Inc. and Random House, Inc., 1949), pp. 48–49. © 1949 by Alfred A. Knopf, Inc.

Public Opinion and American Democracy by V. O. Key, Jr. (New York: Alfred A. Knopf, Inc. and Random House, Inc., 1961), pp. 552–553. © 1961 by V. O. Key, Jr.

The Americans: The National Experience, by Daniel Boorstin (New York: Alfred A. Knopf, Inc. and Random House, Inc., 1965), p. 140. © 1965 by Daniel J. Boorstin.

"The President, the Polls and Vietnam" by Seymour Martin Lipset, *Trans-Action* (September–October 1966): 24. © September 1966 *Society* Magazine by Trans-Action, Inc., New Brunswick, N. J.

Warren, the Man, the Court, the Era, by John D. Weaver (Boston: Little, Brown and Company, 1967), p. 182.

Newsweek (December 6, 1971 and December 13, 1971). © Newsweek, Inc., 1971. Reprinted by permission.

The Collapse of the Third Republic, by William L. Shirer (New York: Simon and Schuster, Inc., 1969), pp. 336–337.

Kevin Phillips as quoted in *New York Times Magazine* (November 14, 1971) and *New York Times* (December 5, 1967). © 1971/1967 by the New York Times Company. Reprinted by permission.

The Sophisticated Poll Watcher's Guide by George Gallup. Reprinted by permission of the author.

Abraham Lincoln as quoted in "Public Opinion in Flux" by Hadley

Acknowledgments

Cantril, *Annals of the American Academy of Political and Social Science* (March 1942): 136.

The Human Dimension: Experiences in Policy Research by Hadley Cantril (New Brunswick, N. J.: Rutgers University Press, 1967), p. 50 and chart.

The Political Beliefs of Americans, by Lloyd A. Free and Hadley Cantril (New Brunswick, N. J.: Rutgers University Press, 1967), p. 40, Table III–4, and Table III–2.

Albert H. Cantril and Charles W. Roll, *Hopes and Fears of the American People* (Washington, D. C.: Potomac Associates, 1971), pp. 37–38; Table 13.

Editorial from *The Evening Star* (March 8, 1972). Courtesy, *The Washington (D. C.) Star.*

Earl Warren: A Political Biography by Leo Katcher, p. 289. © 1967 by Leo Katcher. Reprinted by permission of the William Morris Agency.

A Guide to Public Opinion Polls by George Gallup, 2nd ed. (Princeton: Princeton University Press, 1948), p. 92. © 1948 by Princeton University Press. Reprinted by permission of the publisher.

Robert K. McMillan as quoted in "Candidates Use Opinion Polls to Plan Campaigns for 1972" by Andrew J. Glass, *National Journal* 3 (August 14, 1971): 170–174.

Henry Cabot Lodge: A Biography by William J. Miller (New York: James H. Heineman, Inc., 1967), p. 205.

Public Opinion: Nature, Formation and Role by Harwood L. Childs. © 1965 by Litton Educational Publishing, Inc. Reprinted by permission of Van Nostrand Reinhold Company.

Acknowledgment is made to Walter Lippmann for permission to reprint certain passages from *The Phantom Public,* © copyright 1925 by Walter Lippmann and *Essays in the Public Philosophy,* © copyright 1955 by Walter Lippmann.

Index